Puccini's

MADAMA BUTTERFLY
OPERA CLASSICS LIBRARY™

Edited by Burton D. Fisher
Principal Lecturer, *Opera Journeys Lecture Series*

Opera Journeys ™ Publishing / Coral Gables, Florida

OPERA CLASSICS LIBRARY ™

• Aida • The Barber of Seville • La Bohème • Carmen
• Cavalleria Rusticana • Così fan tutte • Don Giovanni
• Don Pasquale • The Elixir of Love • Elektra
• Eugene Onegin • Exploring Wagner's Ring • Falstaff
• Faust • The Flying Dutchman • Hansel and Gretel
• L'Italiana in Algeri • Julius Caesar • Lohengrin
• Lucia di Lammermoor • Macbeth • Madama Butterfly
• The Magic Flute • Manon • Manon Lescaut
• The Marriage of Figaro • A Masked Ball • The Mikado
• Otello • I Pagliacci • Porgy and Bess • The Rhinegold
• Rigoletto • Der Rosenkavalier • Salome • Samson and Delilah
• Siegfried • The Tales of Hoffmann • Tannhäuser
• Tosca • La Traviata • Il Trovatore • Turandot
• Twilight of the Gods • The Valkyrie

Copyright © 2001 by Opera Journeys Publishing

All rights reserved

All musical notations contained herein are original transcriptions by the authors.
Discography and Videography listings represent selections by the editors.
Printed in the United States of America

WEB SITE: www.operajourneys.com   E MAIL: operaj@bellsouth.net

3rd F1

Contents

Prelude
OPERA CLASSICS LIBRARY's
MADAMA BUTTERFLY

OPERA CLASSICS LIBRARY explores the greatness and magic of Puccini's ingenious masterpiece, *MADAMA BUTTERFLY.*

The *Commentary and Analysis* offers pertinent biographical information about Puccini, the genesis of the opera, its premiere and performance history, and insightful story and character analysis.

The text also contains a *Brief Story Synopsis, Principal Characters in Madama Butterfly,* and a *Story Narrative with Music Highlight Examples,* the latter containing original music transcriptions that are interspersed appropriately within the story's dramatic exposition. In addition, the text includes a *Discography, Videography,* and a *Dictionary of Opera and Musical Terms.*

The *Libretto* has been newly translated by the Opera Journeys staff with specific emphasis on retaining a literal translation, but also with the objective to provide a faithful translation in modern and contemporary English; in this way, the substance of the drama becomes more intelligible. To enhance educational and study objectives, the *Libretto* also contains musical highlight examples interspersed within the drama.

The opera art form is the sum of many artistic expressions: theatrical drama, music, scenery, poetry, dance, acting and gesture. In opera, it is the composer who is the dramatist, using the emotive power of his music to express intense, human conflicts. Words evoke thought, but music provokes feelings; opera's sublime fusion of words, music and all the theatrical arts provides powerful theater, an impact on one's sensibilities that can reach into the very depths of the human soul.

MADAMA BUTTERFLY is certainly a crown jewel among Puccini's glorious operatic inventions; it remains a masterpiece of the lyric theater, and a tribute to the art form and its ingenious composer.

Burton D. Fisher
Editor
OPERA CLASSICS LIBRARY

MADAMA BUTTERFLY

Italian opera in three acts
by
Giacomo Puccini

**Libretto by Luigi Illica and Giuseppe Giacosa,
based on the original story
by John Luther Long,
and the theatrical play adapted by
John Luther Long and David Belasco**

**Premiere at La Scala, Milan
February 1904**

Commentary and Analysis

G iacomo Puccini — 1858 to 1924 — was the heir to Italy's cherished opera icon, Giuseppe Verdi: he became the last superstar of the great Italian opera tradition in which lyricism, melody, and the vocal arts, dominated the art form.

Puccini came from a family of musicians who for generations had been church organists and composers in his native Lucca, Italy, a part of the Tuscany region. His operatic epiphany occurred when he attended a performance of Verdi's *Aida*: at that moment the eighteen year-old budding composer became inspired toward a future in opera. With aid from Queen Margherita of Italy that was supplemented by additional funds from a great uncle, Puccini progressed to the Milan Conservatory where he eventually studied under Amilcare Ponchielli, a renowned musician, teacher, and the composer of *La Gioconda* (1876).

In Milan, Ponchielli became Puccini's mentor and astutely recognized his student's extraordinarily rich orchestral and symphonic imagination and his remarkable harmonic and melodic inventiveness, resources that would become the hallmarks and prime characteristics of Puccini's mature compositional style.

In 1884, at the age of twenty-six, Puccini competed in the publisher Sonzogno's one-act opera contest with his lyric stage work, *Le Villi* ("The Witches"), a phantasmagoric romantic tale about abandoned young women who die of lovesickness. Musically and dramatically, *Le Villi* remains quite a distance from the poignant sentimentalism which later became Puccini's trademark. *Le Villi* lost the contest, however, La Scala agreed to produce it for its following season. But more significantly to Puccini's future career, Giulio Ricordi, the influential publisher, recognized the young composer's talent to write music drama, and lured him from his competitor, Sonzogno.

Puccini became Ricordi's favorite composer, a status that developed into much peer envy, resentfulness, and jealousy among his rivals, as well as from Ricordi's chief publishing competitor, Sonzogno. Nevertheless, Ricordi used his ingenious golden touch to unite composers and librettists, and he proceeded to assemble the best poets and dramatists for his budding star, Puccini.

Ricordi commissioned Puccini to write a second opera, *Edgar* (1889), a melodrama involving a rivalry between two brothers for a seductive Moorish girl that erupts into powerful passions of betrayal and revenge. Its premiere at La Scala was a disappointment, the critics praising Puccini's orchestral and harmonic advancement from *Le Villi,* but in general they considered the work mediocre: even its later condensation from four to three acts could not redeem it or improve its fortunes.

R icordi's faith in his young protege was triumphantly vindicated by the immediate success of Puccini's next opera, *Manon Lescaut* (1893). The genesis of the libretto was itself an operatic melodrama, saturated with feuds and disagreements between its considerable group of librettists who included Ruggiero Leoncavallo, Luigi Illica, Giuseppe Giacosa, Domenico Oliva, Marco Praga, and even Giulio Ricordi himself. The critics and public were unanimous in their praise of Puccini's third opera, and in London, the eminent critic, George Bernard Shaw, noted that in *Manon Lescaut,* "Puccini looks to me more like the heir of Verdi than any of his rivals."

For Puccini's librettos over the next decade, Ricordi secured for him the illustrious team of the scenarist, Luigi Illica, and the poet, playwright, and versifier, Giuseppe Giacosa. The first fruit of their collaboration became *La Bohème* (1896), drawn from Henry Murger's picaresque novel about life among the artists of the Latin Quarter in Paris during the 1830s: *Scènes de la vie de Bohème.*

The critics were strangely cool at *La Bohème's* premiere, several of them finding it a restrained work when compared to the inventive passion and ardor of *Manon Lescaut.* But in spite of negative and sometimes scathing reviews, the public eventually became enamored with the opera, and it would only be in Vienna, where Mahler, openly hostile to Puccini, virtually banned *La Bohème* in favor of Leoncavallo's treatment of the same subject.

After *La Bohème,* Puccini went on to transform Victorien Sardou's play, *La Tosca,* into a sensational, powerful, and thrilling musical action drama, improving on his literary source and providing immortality to its dramatist.

His next opera adapted David Belasco's one-act play, *Madam Butterfly* (1904). At its premiere, the opera experienced what Puccini described as "a veritable lynching," the audience's hostility and denunciation of the composer and his work apparently deliberately engineered by rivals who were jealous of Puccini's success and favored status with Ricordi.

Puccini followed with *La Fanciulla del West* (1910) ("The Girl of the Golden West"), *La Rondine* (1917) ("The Swallow"), the three one-act operas of *Il Trittico* (1918) — *Suor Angelica, Gianni Schicchi* and *Il Tabarro* ("The Cloak), and his final work, *Turandot* (1925), completed posthumously by Franco Alfano under the direction of Arturo Toscanini.

P uccini's musical and dramatic style reflects the naturalistic movement of the "giovane scuola," the late nineteenth century Italian artistic genre called *verismo* — or Realism: these works emphasized swift dramatic action, and were thematically concentrated on the portrayal of human nature in the raw: the portrayal of problems and conflicts of characters in everyday situations. Throughout his career, Puccini identified himself with *verismo,* what he called the "stile mascagnano," the Mascagni style first successfully portrayed in *Cavalleria Rusticana* (1890).

In the Realism genre — *verismo* — no subject was too mundane, no subject was too harsh, and no subject was too ugly; therefore, the plots dealt with hot and heavy passions: sex, seduction, revenge, betrayal, jealousy, murder, and death. In *verismo,* primal passions were the subject of the action: it portrayed the latent animal, the uncivilized savage, and the barbarian part of man's soul: a theatrical confirmation of Darwin's theory that man evolved from primal beast. In Realism and its successors, modernity and *film noire,* man is portrayed as irrational, brutal, crude, cruel, and demonic: *Tosca's* Baron Scarpia, a quintessential example. In Realism, death became the consummation of desire: in Realism, good did not necessarily triumph over evil, and man became viewed purely as a creature of instinct.

Puccini wrote tonal music within the diatonic (whole tone) scale, but within that framework, his style has a strongly personal lyrical signature that is readily identifiable: lush melodies, occasional unresolved dissonances, and daring harmonic and instrumental colors; his writing endows both his vocal and orchestral elements with a soft suppleness, elegance, gentleness, as well as a poignancy.

In all of Puccini's works, leitmotifs — musical fragments and phrases identifying persons and ideas — play a prominent role in providing emotion and reminiscence, however, they are never developed to the systematic symphonic grandeur and integratation of Wagner's music dramas, and are always utilized and exploited for their ultimate dramatic and cohesive effects.

Puccini's dramatic instincts never failed him. He was truly a master stage-craftsman with a consummate knowledge of the demands of the stage and theatrical effects, even, it can be argued, more concerned than Wagner to integrate his music, words, and gestures into a single conceptual unity; perfect examples of Puccini's stage genius are demonstrated in the action ensemble of *Manon Lescaut's* roll-call of the prostitutes, and *Tosca's* "Te Deum." Just like Bellini in *I Puritani,* the music associated with Puccini's heroines — their identifying theme or leitmotif — is heard before the heroine's themselves appear, a brilliant dramatic technique evidenced in the entrances of Tosca, Butterfly, Manon Lescaut, and Mimi.

Puccini had a rare gift for evoking ambience: the bells in Act III of *Tosca,* or the ship's sirens in *Il Tabarro.* In *La Bohème,* his music conveys realistic and minute details of everyday life: Rodolfo's manuscript being burned in the fire; the sound effects from Colline tumbling down the stairs; Schaunard's horn; and the falling snowflakes at the start of Act III. Debussy, no friend to the contemporary school of Italian opera, was prompted to confess to Paul Dukas that he knew of no one who had described the Paris of the age of Louis-Philippe "as well as Puccini in *La Bohème."* Certainly, in three of his operas, *Madama Butterfly, Girl of the Golden West, and Turandot,* Puccini's music brilliantly captures the exotic ambience and atmosphere of their venues.

Puccini, with the exception of his last opera, *Turandot,* was not a composer of ambitious works or grand opera: he did not write works in the stage-spectacle, grand operatic manner of Meyerbeer, Verdi, or Wagner. He commented that "the only music I can make is of small things," acknowledging that his talent and temperament were not suited to works of large design, spectacle, or portrayals of romantic heroism.

Indeed, in *La Bohème* and *Madama Butterfly,* Puccini does not deal with the world of kings, nobles, gods, or heroes, but rather, in their realism, he portrays simple, ordinary people, and the countless little humdrum details of their everyday lives. Certainly, both operas epitomize Puccini's world of "small things," their grandeur not of supercharged passions evolving from world-shattering events, but rather from moments of poignant emotions and pathos. Ultimately, in the writing of dramas filled with emotion and passion, Puccini had few equals in inventing a personal lyricism that portrayed intimate humanity with sentimentalism and beauty.

Puccini's writing for both voice and orchestra is rich and elegant. His supreme talent was his magic for inventive melody, which he expressed in combinations of outstanding instrumental coloration and harmonic texture: a signature that is so individual that it is recognized immediately. Puccini's memorable arias are endlessly haunting: one leaves a Puccini opera performance, but the music never leaves the listener.

Puccini once described himself as a passionate hunter of wildfowl, an inveterate hunter of attractive women, and an obsessive hunter of good librettos. His hunt for a libretto in the early 1900s was resolved when he discovered the Belasco-Long play *Madam Butterfly.* David Belasco was a theatrical icon, comparable to our contemporary theatrical notables such as David Merrick or Joseph Papp. At the turn of the nineteenth century, Belasco was at the height of his fame as a playwright and theatrical producer. For Belasco, the *Madam Butterfly* story was perfectly suited to his stage flamboyance: its inherent exoticism provided a great opportunity for colorful and innovative sets, costumes, and special effects.

Belasco's particular forte was his unique ability and special ingenuity to create illusion and atmosphere through cunning manipulation of lighting and scenery. He proved his brilliant theatrical creativity in the first scene of his play, *Madam Butterfly:* his curtain rose to a series of illuminated screens depicting in turn a rice-field, a garden of cherry blossoms, a snow-capped volcano, and a sunset, devices he later employed in his play *Girl of the Golden West,* which later became another inspiration for a Puccini opera. These effects might appear naive, flashy, showy, and ornate to the theatergoer of today, but at that time, they were hailed as the dawn of modern stage technique.

In effect, Belasco wed into the theater new techniques that would later be incorporated into the nascent film industry. His greatest coup, one that earned him the epithet "wizard of the stage," occurred in *Madam Butterfly* during the geisha's "Night Vigil" scene: Butterfly's overnight anticipation of Pinkerton's return. In order to mark the passage of time, night turned into day in a scene that lasted fourteen minutes: Belasco manufactured a series of changing effects on the open stage: dusk changed with the gradual appearance of the stars; the break of dawn was accompanied by the chirping of birds; and finally, there was a sunrise. Belasco himself concluded that he had conceived this scene as a challenge to himself, considering it "my most successful effort in appealing to the imagination of those who have sat before my stage."

Belasco's play was a raving success in both New York and London, and in 1900, Puccini attended a London performance of *Madam Butterfly*. Even though Puccini understood no English, he immediately fell in love with the pathetic plight of the Japanese geisha heroine. His emotional response to what was for him mime, was excellent proof of the remarkable clarity and theatrical dramatic effectiveness of the plot. At an earlier time, Puccini had a similar response upon seeing Sardou's *La Tosca*, heard by him in the French, which he also did not understand.

Belasco's *Madam Butterfly* and the heroine's fate struck deep chords in Puccini, but it was specifically her tragic suicide-death that mesmerized and inspired the composer. To heighten the pathos of the story, Belasco and the originator of the story, John Luther Long, modified Long's version; in the original, Pinkerton never sets eyes on Butterfly after his desertion, and she and the child simply disappear. So, to emphasize the poignancy of the drama they added Butterfly's suicide and Pinkerton's return with his new American wife to retrieve the child.

With this revision, the agony of Butterfly's conflict became more profound. When Butterfly finally realizes that she has been abandoned, she faces three alternatives: first, marriage to Prince Yamadori; second, resumption of her former profession, and third, death — her most courageous choice. It is Butterfly's decision to resolve her conflict through self-annihilation that transforms the story into a grave tragedy and elevates her to true heroine status.

The new dramatic conclusion to the Belasco-Long *Madam Butterfly* fit perfectly into Puccini's tragic heroine images: within his unconscious, simple or erotic love was sinful (Manon, Mimi, Tosca, and Butterfly), as opposed to saintly love (Puccini's exalted mother). In effect, the composer punishes these sinful women in agonizing and almost sadistic deaths that theoretically represent subconscious manifestations of his raging mother complex.

After viewing a performance of *Madam Butterfly* in London, Puccini met Belasco and Long backstage, and with impassioned tears he begged them for the rights to transform *Madam Butterfly* into an opera. Belasco agreed, but would later cynically comment that it was impossible to negotiate with an impulsive Italian who was in tears, and who also had his arms threateningly around his neck.

After Puccini succeeded in winning the *Madam Butterfly* rights, he gathered his favorite poets, Illica and Giacosa, the librettists for his earlier successes, *Manon Lescaut, La Bohème,* and *Tosca*. Puccini proceeded to plunge into his mysterious fascination with the character of *Madam Butterfly*, the next entry into his gallery of tragic heroines.

Madama Butterfly provided Puccini with an opportunity to musically characterize Far Eastern exoticisms, ethnicity, ambience and atmosphere — as well as American and Western characteristics. In pursuing his musical sketches for *Madama Butterfly*, Puccini — as he would again do 20 years later for the Chinese ambience of *Turandot* — pored over collections of Japanese folk music, records, books on Japanese customs, religious ceremonies and architecture; the ultimate result was that he became an astute student of Oriental ethnography.

The underlying theme that is the core of the plight of Puccini's geisha heroine, *Madama Butterfly,* or Cio-Cio-San, is a collision of cultures. Japanese and oriental themes particularly captivated European opera and operetta composers of the late nineteenth century: Meyerbeer's *L'Africaine* (1865), Delibes's *Lakme* (1883), Sullivan's *The Mikado* (1885), Messager's *Madame Chrysantheme* (1893), Jones's *The Geisha* (1896), Mascagni's *Iris* (1898).

The clash of two cultures, the incompatibility of East and West, and by implication, the white race's arrogant superiority, form the underlying engine of all of these dramas: the heroines belong to non-European races; they all fall in love with a white man which serves to offend their own racial customs and traditions; and all of their lovers desert them to return to their native lands.

The specific Long *Madam Butterfly* story owes most of its provenance to Pierre Loti, a French naval officer whose 1887 autobiographical novel *Madame Chrysantheme* set the fashion for the use of Japanese subjects in Western literature and in opera. In *Madame Chrysanthemum,* Loti's exotic poetic touches, his aromas and moods, his oriental atmospheric impressions, his depictions of that delicate fragile world of tiny objects and minute details, were all cast against the background of an exotic land of cherry blossoms, chrysanthemums, geishas, and the samurai. From Loti's European lens, he said that "in describing this land, its culture, and its people, one is tempted to use the word 'tiny' six times a line."

Some years later, John Luther Long wrote a sensational magazine story that appeared serialized in the American Century Magazine, and was titled *Madam Butterfly.* Long claimed that he was relating a true episode about a Japanese geisha who married an American naval officer under Japanese law, bore him a child, and was later abandoned by the American; the Japanese wife was forced to give-up the child to the officer and his new American wife.

The authenticity of the story was supposedly confirmed to Puccini by the wife of Italy's Ambassador to Japan, although Long admittedly modeled most his story on the much read novel of Pierre Loti. Loti's heroine was Ki-Hou-San, meaning Chrysanthemum; Long changed it to Cho-Cho-San, and then incongruously "Englished" the title to *Madam Butterfly.*

In Long's magazine story, he convincingly captured the exotic and strangely foreign atmosphere of Japan at the turn of the nineteenth century. Western civilization considered the Far East legendary and romantic; it was a time when they were gradually being brought into contact with the orient through commerce and colonial expansion. Long's *Madam Butterfly* heroine was a bit crude, however, his specific intention was to realistically portray Japanese life. In Long, Butterfly is a silly lovesick girl who speaks "pidgin" English, tries to "go all American" by insisting that "no one shall speak anytin' but dose Uni'd Sta'es languages in dis Lef-ten-ant Pik-ker-ton's house," and that her marriage to an American officer "make me mos' bes' happy female woman in Japan – mebby in that whole worl' – w'at you thing?"

The American naval officer's characterization which Long adapted was modeled after Loti himself. Pinkerton is offensive and arrogant, a callous and fatuous practical joker, a cynic and racist adventurer with a devil-may-care attitude, and one who fancies himself in the role of a modern Pygmalion; he is the self-proclaimed lord and master over his geisha. The American counsel Sharpless makes the most profound comment about Pinkerton in Long's story, "It was exactly in his line to take this dainty, vivid, eager and formless material, Cho Cho San, and mould it to his most wantonly whimsical wish." Sharpless wryly adds that "it was perhaps fortunate for Butterfly that his country had need of him so soon after his marriage."

The latter part of the nineteenth and early twentieth centuries were periods of intense colonialism in Asia by American and European powers; as the Industrial Revolution flourished, the Western powers were seeking to plunder untapped resources in order to fuel their industrial economies. The United States joined in colonial acquisitions by initially seizing the Hawaiian and Philippine Islands.

In 1898, the Americans declared the Open Door Policy, in effect, a doctrine of equal opportunity intended to conveniently served as an excuse to rape China. The Chinese empire at that time was an easy target for exploitation because it was internally poor, weak, impotent and uncoordinated; its bureaucratic autocracy was entirely out of touch with its millions of peasants, who, in turn, were tyrannized by the landlord classes. The Chinese victims of this foreign exploitation expressed their opposition through the "Righteous Harmonious Fists" Movement, the rebellion and resistance to foreign intervention and exploitation that became known as the Boxer Rebellion.

The Japanese also looked to China for resources to fuel their newly industrialized economy. Japanese racial superiority toward the Chinese added an additional excuse to their actions. In effect, the British, French, German, Americans — and the Japanese —were allies with one purpose: the exploitation of China and its natural resources.

The period in which the *Butterfly* story takes place was during the Japanese Meiji dynasty (1868-1912). Japan had been secluded for centuries, but became obsessed to modernize, and determined to build their economy and military ever since Commodore Perry entered Japan by force in 1853. Japan did not want to become humbled by the "barbarian" foreigners like China, so they transformed themselves, reorganized their privileged society, and sold their silk so they could build western style industry, and ultimately, their military-industrial complex. But in their process of progress and modernization, they embraced everything Western: from trains to clothes, haircuts, literature, and that explains so much of their love of the West and America that is portrayed throughout the *Butterfly* story.

At the end of the nineteenth century, Japan lowered its cultural and economic barriers to the West and became an ally of the United States. Part of that policy was to permit an American naval presence in Japan. The American warship in the *Madama Butterfly* story, the Abraham Lincoln, was assigned to intelligence surveillance of the Chinese coast; the Japanese made the port of Nagasaki available to their American allies for rendezvous and fueling.

To further encourage friendship with their European and American allies, the Japanese allowed foreigners to avail themselves of Japanese women by providing them with the same legal rights accorded Japanese men: foreigners could enter into temporary marriages with Japanese women with a convenient arrangement whereby the marriage could be terminated on the expiration of the "husband's" leave. In effect, this Japanese law — perhaps an anathema to modern day humanists and feminists — allowed Westerners to marry Japanese women with the singular option that the men could annul the marriage contract at any time — of course the wife was bound for life (999 years in the *Butterfly* story).

Both parties would enter these marriages in the spirit of *carpe diem:* there was no tragedy, regret or remorse after the husband departed and rejoined his ship. In Pierre Loti's *Madame Chrysanthemum*, the precursor to the Long-Belasco *Madam Butterfly* story, the naval officer's farewell is dispelled simply with money, the heroine meticulously counting coins that represent her parting present, and testing them with a hammer and the competence and dexterity of an old moneylender.

Goro is the first character who appears in the opera: he is a Japanese "Figaro," a factotum, or "do-it-all, that rare combination of interpreter, busybody, matchmaker, producer of the bride, as well as the real estate agent for Pinkerton's house rental. Pinkerton's special orders to Goro were that the rented house was to be remote and specially fitted with screen locks in order to keep Butterfly isolated, in particular, kept away from the prying eyes of her family; a family he hated.

With the arrival of Sharpless, a friend of Pinkerton as well as the American Consul in Nagasaki, Puccini's music becomes more familiarly Westernized: broad and expansive music that is intended to portray Sharpless's diverse character: at times grave and pompous, at times boring and bland, but always representing a good natured and gentle man.

Thanks to Goro, Pinkerton purchased his bride Butterfly for 100 yen. Butterfly will later comment that she will be very frugal, because she knows how expensive Pinkerton's purchase had been. Pinkerton raves to Sharpless about the wonderful Japanese marriage contract he has made, elastic and cancelable by him at anytime, however, never cancelable by Butterfly.

Pinkerton's revelations fuel the drama and set the tragedy in motion. Pinkerton is a man of dubious integrity. He is a heartless, arrogant, and callous scoundrel who arouses revulsion; opera's quintessential cad. He is clearly the "ugly American," an awestruck adventurer and evil tool of the Western preoccupation with imperialism and colonialism that pervaded the latter part of the nineteenth century.

Pinkerton rants about white racial superiority, and that his marriage to his child bride will not be a sacred and holy matrimony, but rather a momentary, trivial, and irrelevant pursuit. He admits to his irrational physical attraction to Butterfly, an addiction to her mysterious and exotic oriental charm that has captivated, intoxicated, and fascinated him.

Pinkerton's aria, "Dovunque al mondo lo Yankee vagabondo" ("All over the world, on business or pleasure, the Yankee scorns danger"), is a sort of male chauvinist ditty about macho American males who travel the world picking, choosing, and conquering women. If anything, Pinkerton certainly does not endear himself to modern day feminists or to anti-colonialists.

When Sharpless interrupts Pinkerton with his voice of caution to advise him that his free and easy hedonistic philosophy of pleasure can be dangerous and bring damage and despair to a tender heart, his caution goes unheeded. Pinkerton is an arrogant man who insulates himself from tragedy. He denounces Sharpless's humane caution by insulting his age: "Men of your age look on life gloomily," concluding with a final toast to the folks at home, "And to the day of my real marriage to an American wife." If anything, Pinkerton's revelations place our sympathies with Butterfly even before we meet her.

Pinkerton's opening aria "Dovunque al mondo" contains some musical plagiarism with the opening strains from the "Star Spangled Banner," an ingenious example of Puccini's mastery of exotic punctuation. The climactic finale, underscored with the words, "America Forever," are intended to arouse our hostility toward Pinkerton's chauvinism, as well as toward the morality of Western colonialism and imperialism.

Butterfly's entrance in the first act is perhaps one of the most magical and dramatic transitions in all opera, an ironic contrast to Pinkerton's revelations. She climbs the hill accompanied by friends, family, and her wedding entourage, and her words and spirit revel in this glorious wedding day: "I am the happiest girl in Japan and all the world," and, "I have arrived to answer the call of love."

Her entrance music is elegant, simple, and pulsating, all very simply based on a four-note phrase that ascends and rises chromatically, climaxing in a magnificently arching, lush, and sensuous musical finale. The entrance music, the "Happiness Motive," is the signature music of the opera, becoming a leitmotif identifying Butterfly's "happiness," a stark contrast to the tragedy that will overcome her. Puccini later integrates this music into the "Love Duet" ending Act I, and Butterfly's triumphant exultation in Act II when she believes that Pinkerton has returned. The theme is also heard in musical variations and transformations that are intended to capture various states of mind: Butterfly's expression of nostalgia for her past happiness.

Butterfly is the center of the whole drama, her character growing in a continuous and consistent line from a child-bride in Act I, to the agonizing harsh realities that eventually transform her into a tragic heroine at the end of the opera.

Butterfly is fifteen years old, a teenager with very mature instincts, and a geisha by profession, who sings and dances for clients: in Japan, according to Butterfly, an honorable profession. In a contemporary context, she would be considered perhaps a "go-go" dancer at a strip club. She is not, as a misconception, a prostitute, although on the geisha ladder of success, prostitution should not be discounted as a future possibility.

Butterfly arrives at her wedding bearing many past sorrows. Two tragic events occurred in her short life that had forced her to become a geisha. Firstly, her family's home and property were destroyed by a tsunami: a typhoon. Secondly, her father sided with the emperor in subduing a rebellion, but failed in his assigned mission. To preserve his honor, he committed hara-kiri, the Japanese ritual suicide that was in accordance with the emperor's "invitation." In Long's original story, it is emphasized that Butterfly's mother ordered her to marry Pinkerton so that she would be able to contribute money for clothes and food to her family.

So Butterfly has "arrived." Her marriage to an American naval officer will provide her with status and security. In effect, she has climbed the prevailing social ladder and achieved upward mobility. Butterfly is a lady now, no longer obligated to work as a geisha.

Musically, *Madama Butterfly* gave Puccini the opportunity to create a collage of exotic melodies and themes. His intent was not to plagiarize Japanese ethnic music, but rather to capture oriental color and atmosphere through musical vignettes. There is no overture or prelude. Puccini's opening music immediately portrays a sense of agitation and excitement, as the atmosphere conveys the anticipation of a Japanese wedding event. The opening music is intended to convey western stereotypes of oriental culture: the patter of tiny feet, and the quaint, fussy, doll-like characters of the Eastern world.

After Butterfly's entrance, Puccini quotes many original Japanese tunes. For example, the Japanese "National Anthem" is used to announce the arrival of the Imperial Commissioner and the Official Registrar; the "Cherry Blossom Song" provides the musical background when Butterfly shows Pinkerton her various knickknacks and possessions, and the Japanese song "Nihon Bashi" is heard when Butterfly's friends offer their congratulations. In Act II, an authentic Japanese prayer melody underscores Suzuki's prayer, and the Japanese popular song, "My Prince," underscores Yamadori's entrance music.

In order to add an exotic color to the musical ambience, there is authentic Japanese music written in the pentatonic scale, the five-note scale particular to oriental music. However, when the score shakes off its Japanese trimmings and becomes truly Italian, or Puccinian in texture, the contrast forces the pulse to quicken, and the senses to respond.

In Act I, Pinkerton and Butterfly step aside to be alone, the scene underscored by the beautiful "Happiness Motive" music from Butterfly's entrance. Butterfly tells Pinkerton a secret, cautioning Pinkerton that not her family, and particularly not her uncle, the Buddhist priest called the Bonze, may discover her secret actions of yesterday. Butterfly visited the Christian Mission, was baptized, and adopted a new religion: Pinkerton's religion. She believes that her conversion to Christianity was a supreme act of love and faith, all done in the hope that it would make her new husband happy.

In Butterfly's conception, both she and Pinkerton will worship and pray together in the same church and to the same god: wherever fate leads her, she will follow her destiny with her new husband and her new god, convinced that her new husband's kindly god will always protect her and hear her prayers. Butterfly has decided to discard her culture, her relatives, and her ancestors. To prove this to Pinkerton, she throws away her sacred ancestral images, those little dolls symbolizing her ancestors' souls. In effect, Butterfly has ceded her ancient heritage and culture, an act of blasphemy that will later lead to renunciation and ostracism from her family.

At the conclusions of the "Conversion aria," Butterfly declares her devotyed love for Pinkerton: "Amore mio " ("My only love"), but she cuts herself short, fearful of being overheard by her relatives. Puccini emphasizes her fright, ending the aria with a decisive fortissimo that is musically underscored by the "Suicide motive," a pentatonic theme heard earlier when Goro related the story about Butterfly's father's obedience to the Mikado's "invitation" to perform an honorable death through hara kiri.

The wedding celebration is noisily interrupted by the violently raging and infuriated shouts of the Bonze, Butterfly's uncle, the Buddhist priest. The Bonze has learned that Butterfly converted to Christianity and relinquished her sacred ancestral religion.

He interrogates Butterfly: "What were you doing at the Mission yesterday?" And he announces to all present: "She has renounced us all!" The Bonze curses Butterfly, damns her soul, and condemns her to eternal punishment; Butterfly has been renounced for heresy and blasphemy.

The relatives likewise join in and renounce Butterfly: by deserting her gods, Butterfly has in effect denounced her people. In this era of Japanese history, the country is a theocracy in which the state and religion are united. The Bonze's curse represents excommunication, and his curse will haunt Butterfly throughout her forthcoming ordeal of abandonment and loneliness.

Pinkerton intervenes and condemns the Bonze for his intrusion, concluding that all of the Bonze's parroting is ridiculous nonsense. The Bonze departs with the wedding guests, and all join him in shouting to Butterfly, "we renounce you." The "Renunciation motive" is a chromatic theme that repeats throughout the opera: as a leitmotif, it is a musical reminder of Butterfly's guilt.

Butterfly is in tears, and covers her ears so as not to hear her family's shouts of renunciation. She has been rejected, and she begins to perceive the gravity of her ostracism. She trembles in fear, continuously repeating that she is an outcast, cursed and renounced by her people. Pinkerton consoles her with unusual sentiments of tenderness, understanding, as well as reassurances of his love for her.

Evening descends. Butterfly enters the house to change into the bride's traditional sacred white wedding garments. Together, Butterfly and Pinkerton rejoice in their overflowing love. The music alternates with a collision of themes: the Bonze's "Renunciation motive," and Butterfly's "Happiness motive." Fear and happiness are the ironies that musically collide in the "Love Duet."

The "Love Duet" is indeed an ecstatic moment of operatic bliss. Almost childlike, Butterfly fears to speak of her love for Pinkerton, but Pinkerton assures her that love gives life. The final chords of their duet are dissonant and tonally unresolved, Puccini's musical way of telling us that this blissful appearance of consummated love is not resolved.

In Long's original story, Pinkerton and Butterfly marry and live in New York for several months. In the opera, after the wedding night, Pinkerton leaves for intelligence service on the China coast. In Long's story, he indeed remained — a few months perhaps.

In Act II, Puccini transforms the ecstatic rapture from the "Love Duet" toward the gradual destruction of Butterfly's will: the development of her pathetic tragedy. Butterfly, until the very end of the tragedy, is in denial, a profound tension that is created by her invincible will and loyalty to Pinkerton, and her conviction that Pinkerton has not deserted her. She lives in a state of delusion, undaunted in her hope and expectation that he will return. But slowly, her developing consciousness forces her to face the horrible reality that she has been betrayed and abandoned.

As Act II opens, it is three years after the Act I wedding and Butterfly is now 18 year old. Pinkerton has not written to Butterfly since their wedding night, and her money is running out. Butterfly survives solely on hope and expectation, always resolute, unwavering, and undaunted in her spirit, a blind faith and conviction that her husband will return.

Suzuki prays for Pinkerton's return, but Butterfly condemns Suzuki's prayers to those "fat and ugly" Japanese gods, proclaiming that her new god, her adopted god, the god of her beloved Pinkerton, is more kindly, and that he answers the prayers of those who adore him. Suzuki reminds Butterfly that foreign husbands never return after they have departed, but Butterfly is firm in her faith and conviction that Pinkerton will indeed return to her, an affirmation that her love remains as ardent and steadfast as on the day they first met. Intrepid in her belief, she commands the doubting Suzuki to say he will return.

Butterfly is inspired with a vision, her imagination anticipating Pinkerton's return. In the aria "Un bel di" ("One beautiful day"), she fantasizes a scenario describing her joy and ecstasy as she envisions Pinkerton climbing up the hill.

In the aria, a pentatonic musical line underscores the words "s'avvia per la collina" ("in the distance a tiny speck will climb the hill"), the same music that will ironically repeat at the end of Act III when Butterfly tells Sharpless that Pinkerton should return for the child in a half hour.

The aria "Un bel di" affirms Butterfly's faith, as well as her despair.

Butterfly suffers from many delusions, all products of Pinkerton's inventions. Pinkerton totally transformed Butterfly. At the same time, he became a substitute for everything sacred in her life: Butterfly's "ancestor-at-large." In this Japanese culture, ancestors — living and dead — were the sole link to eternal life. Pinkerton, by inventing himself in Butterfly's mind as a godly creature, provided Butterfly with a new road to eternal salvation; a new religion, and his own plan of salvation.

Butterfly surely knows that in order to divorce according to Japanese law, all Pinkerton need do was tell her to leave. Since Pinkerton did not do this, Butterfly remains deluded and believes that his return is inevitable. Pinkerton manufactured his own style of Western education: he created a scenario that taught Butterfly that if they were to divorce, they would have to physically go to America, further elaborating that in America, once married, divorce is a virtually impossible process that involves many years in courthouses with the additional possibility that one could go to jail. To Butterfly, who has been throughly brainwashed by Pinkerton, all of these Western cultural and legal assumptions were proof that she was still married to Pinkerton, and that in time he would return to her.

Sharpless, who had not seen Butterfly since the wedding three years ago, arrives with a letter from Pinkerton. The letter actually informs Sharpless that Pinkerton married an American wife, an event foretold in Act I when Pinkerton offered a toast to his real American marriage. The scene is intended to further stimulate our sense of moral indignation and outrage at the Yankee vagabond. In Pinkerton's letter, he instructs Sharpless to "buy off" Butterfly, and ironically suggests that she certainly would not remember him after three years. Sharpless tries to read Pinkerton's letter to Butterfly, but Butterfly frustrates him, continually interrupting him with childish digressions. Butterfly asks Sharpless when the robins build their nests in America, an inquiry based on Pinkerton's promise that he would return in that happy season "when robins are building their nests."

Sharpless makes valiant attempts to read the letter to Butterfly, but he is interrupted by the arrival of Prince Yamadori and Goro. Yamadori's music is broad and arching, almost grandly "Tristanesque" in its range. Yamadori, according to the original Long story, is one of those wealthy pensioned Princes of Japan, a fascinating matrimonial object who is well traveled, speaks fluent English, has a permanent residence in New York, and undertakes occasional pleasure tips to Japan.

Prince Yamadori is a Japanese "playboy," but he is now one of Goro's clients who has divorced all of his wives because he is madly in love with Butterfly; he tells Butterfly that he is now prepared to swear eternal faithfulness to her. But Butterfly is repulsed by his promises of salvation and contemptuously rejects him, declaring proudly that she is a married woman, a woman married under American law, who wants to remain faithful to her husband in accordance with that law. Butterfly relishes the opportunity to vindicate oppressed Japanese womanhood. At the same time, she does a little bashing and condemns Japanese law and its inherent chauvinism, the law that allows a man to turn his wife out if he is so inclined. Butterfly proudly proclaims that in her country, judges protect wives.

In Long's story, Yamadori's visit was initiated by Goro who persuaded Butterfly to let Yamadori visit her. It was a "look-see," an inspection which she consented to in lieu of receiving traditional presents. But actually, Butterfly was lonely and just wanted a little attention, or perhaps it was an ego trip or an opportunity for vindication, or even an opportunity to brag about her American marriage. After all, Pinkerton made her a refinement of a Japanese product, and he did promise her that one day — in the original Long story — they would live happily ever after, move to America, and live in a castle.

Yamadori departs in frustration, spurned and rejected by Butterfly. After he leaves, Sharpless again tries to read Pinkerton's letter to Butterfly, and is again perplexed and frustrated by her childish interruptions. Each time he starts reading, Butterfly hears only what she wants to hear. She interrupts him with her own interpretation of its content and believes that the letter announces Pinkerton's imminent return.

The "Letter Scene" music that underscores Sharpless' attempt to read Pinkerton's letter to Butterfly will return during *Butterfly*'s "Night Vigil," the scene separating Acts II and III in which night turns to day.

S harpless is overcome with angst, and is compelled to tell Butterfly the truth: he can spare her no longer. Angrily, but with almost fatherly affection, he builds up his courage to ask Butterfly what she would do if Pinkerton should never return to her.

Butterfly becomes completely transformed, stunned, and shocked, as if struck by a death blow. She becomes childlike. She stammers. Then she explains two courses that might remain to her: to return to being a geisha and entertain again with song and dance, or better, to die, the words and music colliding and conveying an ominous sense of forthcoming disaster.

Sharpless tries to lighten the tension by suggesting that Butterfly marry Yamadori, but his proposal merely prompts Butterfly to explode into a fit of contempt and outrage. Butterfly arises from her chair and shows Sharpless the door, but then takes hold of herself, calms down, and becomes apologetic, explaining to Sharpless that her outburst was because he offended and wounded her. Suddenly, Butterfly suspects defeat. In an outburst, she screams that "he has forgotten me"; the orchestral music is fortissimo, ironically underscored with a thunderous rendering of the "Happiness motive."

The drama has reached its turning point and key climactic moment. Butterfly goes into the adjoining room and returns with her three-year old child: his name, "dolore" ("trouble" "pain" or "sorrow"), a name that will be changed to "gioia" ("joy"). Long explains that every Japanese baby starts life with a temporary name, so Butterfly too planned to rename the child "gioia" in celebration of the father's return.

Pointing to the boy, Butterfly asks Sharpless: "Can this be forgotten?" Sharpless was unaware of the child and is a bit stunned. He questions whether the baby is Pinkerton's. Butterfly points to the boy's Caucasian features, his blue eyes and fair hair, all obvious assurances that he is Pinkerton's son.

Butterfly sings to her son, "Che tua madre" ("That your mother"), a somber lament revealing that she would rather die than face the dishonor and shame of being deserted and forced to return to geisha life: singing, dancing, and begging for money. Puccini's underlying music recalls the "Suicide" motive in the pentatonic scale..

According to the Long story, Butterfly never wanted to tell Pinkerton about the child. Pinkerton had deluded her with his fabrications about Western life and culture, and as such, Butterfly believed that if Pinkerton knew about the child, he would desert his country and "be in big trouble with the President of the United States." She actually believed that Pinkerton occupied an important position in the affairs of his country, being, as she said, "under special patronage to the President and the Goddess of Liberty." These naive ideas that Pinkerton so capriciously planted in Butterfly's mind, aptly explain her naive misconceptions, as well as her idolization of Pinkerton as some type of divine creature.

A saddened Sharpless departs, promising Butterfly that he will tell Pinkerton about the child. Butterfly, now alone with her child, pours out her love for him, assuring him that they will be avenged, their pride redeemed, and that Pinkerton will indeed return and take them away to his own country.

A loud cannon shot is heard from the harbor: the cannon shot, the traditional announcement of the arrival of an American warship. The background music reechoes the aria "Un bel di," Butterfly's fantasy about Pinkerton's return. Butterfly trembles in excitement. With telescope in hand, she identifies the flag and colors of the warship Abraham Lincoln, Pinkerton's ship.

For Butterfly, the agony of waiting is over. In exultation — to the musical themes of the "Happiness motive," "Love Duet," and the "Star Spangled Banner" — Butterfly explodes in triumph. Pinkerton has indeed arrived, and she was right all the time. Butterfly now expresses her contempt and disdain for being renounced by her people and relatives, as well as her scorn at Yamadori's arrogance and Goro's scandalous lies. It is Butterfly's triumphal moment of victory, and a magnificent musico-dramatic climax: the "Happiness" theme resounds in a full orchestra. Everyone told Butterfly that all hope had vanished, but her love and faith have prevailed. Butterfly has been vindicated.

Butterfly and Suzuki are euphoric and ecstatic as they celebrate this moment, an event anticipated for three years. They adorn the house with flowers so that Pinkerton will see "springtime glory." Butterfly comments that it was her devotion and tears that saturated the earth to bear those flowers.

As the sun begins to set, Butterfly dresses herself in her wedding obi so that she may greet Pinkerton as he remembered her in their last moments of happiness. Butterfly looks into a mirror and laments how time and her grieving have changed her; her smile is now saddened, and she has aged.

Together with the child and Suzuki, Butterfly maintains a vigil throughout the night. She punches three little holes in the soshi screen so they can watch for Pinkerton. Suzuki, Butterfly, and the boy, all rigid, statuesque, and motionless, settle down for their "Night Vigil," poised facing the harbor. The boy and Suzuki fall asleep, but Butterfly remains awake all night.

The orchestra ironically repeats the musical theme from the "Letter Scene": the music is seemingly a lullaby, but it is fused with ominous appearances and variations of the "Renunciation motive," further emphasizing Butterfly's pathetic futility and ominous fate. The "Night Vigil," night becoming day, the transition from Act II to Act III, was one of Puccini's primary inspirations from Belasco's play, a moment that provided the composer with an opportunity to invent a host of musical imagery: like Belasco's play, day dawning, birds chirping and the sounds of morning.

Puccini originally wrote Acts II and III combined as one act, because he feared that in separating them, he would be destroying the dramatic continuity of night turning into day. As such, his original second act comprised 1 hour and 20 minutes, even though he was duly warned that its length could prove disastrous. Nevertheless, Puccini resisted the advice, so at its premiere, Butterfly's third act was presented as part of Act II. Its length certainly contributed to the premiere fiasco, but later Puccini divided the original Act II into 2 parts — Acts II and III — the format in which it is usually performed in modern times.

Pinkerton has been told by Sharpless that he has fathered a child. Act III deals with Pinkerton, his new American wife, Kate, and their determination to rescue the child from the perceived squalor of Japanese life; their intention is to bring the child to America. Since there is no custody battle, the father, under the then existing Japanese law, exercises his rights by will and wish.

Pinkerton and Sharpless arrive and find Suzuki. They explain their desire to "rescue" the child, and Kate Pinkerton begs Suzuki's support in order to ease Butterfly's pain. Suzuki's protestations are futile, and she pleads with them that Butterfly should be spared the agony whereby a mother is commanded to give up her child.

Pinkerton's return to Japan becomes traumatic for him. He reflects on the bitterness of the flowers which symbolize to him a faded love. He is sad, and even senses death filling the air. Pinkerton has now awakened to recognize his selfishness and begs forgiveness.

Now overcome with emotion, he cannot bear his own guilt any longer and admits his remorse. Sharpless reminds him that he prophesied this tragedy, but in his arrogance, Pinkerton had been deaf to his warnings.

Pinkerton's aria, "Addio fiorito asil" ("Farewell sanctuary of flowers"), was added by Puccini after the debacle of the Butterfly premiere. "Addio fiorito asil" is a stunning operatic moment: it represents Pinkerton's grand apology and lament, a moment of transformation in which he admits his grave and fatal errors, concluding that peace will never return to him, and that he will always be haunted and tormented by guilt. He leaves abruptly, unable to face the woman he has betrayed: his final words, "Son vil" ("I am vile.")

Butterfly enters, shouting "he's here, he's here," childishly suspecting that Pinkerton is hiding and playing a game with her. But as Butterfly searches in vain, she notices a woman in the garden: the woman is Kate Pinkerton. All are silent.

Reality overcomes Butterfly. At first she is shocked. She asks about the lady in the garden? No one answers. Then her faithful Suzuki's tears reveal to Butterfly the bitter truth. Butterfly's intuitive suspicions are now transformed into the horrible realization of her tragic fate.

Butterfly asks Suzuki if Pinkerton is alive, and Suzuki confirms that he is. She asks if they told her that Pinkerton will not return, and Suzuki is silent. Suzuki then admits to Butterfly that he will not return to her, but he has indeed arrived in Nagasaki. Butterfly becomes frightened when she again notices Kate, the blonde lady in the garden, but Suzuki defends Kate as the innocent cause of Butterfly's grief and misfortune.

Butterfly intuitively deduces that the woman in the garden is Pinkerton's wife. She concludes to herself that her situation is hopeless and that they will take everything from her. Sharpless tries to reason with her that if she gives the child to Pinkerton, the boy would have a brighter future, but Butterfly indignantly protests that a mother cannot be asked to give up her child.

Butterfly finally faces the horrible truth. With obedient resignation, she resolves to obey their wishes. With a pathetic sense of dignity, she decides to yield. Butterfly will give up her son, but she adds the proviso that she will only give the boy to Pinkerton himself.

Suzuki escorts Kate and Sharpless out. Butterfly is emotionally distraught and at the point of collapse. She asks Suzuki to make the room darker and remove all the brightness associated with joy and springtime. Afterwards, she commands Suzuki to go out and play with the child.

With Suzuki's sobs heard in the background, Butterfly kneels before the Buddha. In conclusive moves, she removes her father's dagger from the shrine, kisses the blade, and reads its inscribed words, words that represent the essence and soul of her culture: "Con onor muore chi non puo serbar vita con onore" ("One shall die with honor who no longer can live his life with honor.")

A door opens and Suzuki pushes the child towards Butterfly. Butterfly drops the dagger, and hugs and kisses the baby. Puccini specifically indicates the mood of his score at this very moment: "con grande sentimento affanosamente agitato" ("with great and agitated feeling"), Puccini's musical direction to express Butterfly's agonizaing surrender.

Butterfly sings a heart-wrenching farewell to her son, asking him to look at her face and remember her features. In Butterfly's culture, she was taught how to die, yet Pinkerton taught her that the essence of life was love. With all lost, suicide — an honorable death — has become her only alternative. The dagger she holds, in her culture, is a soul; Butterfly has returned to her Japanese culture.

Butterfly seats the boy on a stool, bandages his eyes, gives him an American flag and a doll, and then ushers him outside. She seizes the dagger and goes behind the screen. The dagger is heard falling. Butterfly emerges from behind the screen, tottering and smiling feebly.

Pinkerton is heard anxiously calling: "Butterfly, Butterfly, Butterfly." Butterfly falls, and dies. The piercing, thundering dissonance of Puccini's last chords create an effect of numbness; the chords leave one traumatized with a sense of outrage, pity, sympathy, compassion, and certainly indignation.

*M*adama Butterfly has remained the basis for many theatrical productions highlighting the cultural clash of East and West. The Broadway musical *Miss Saigon*, updates the *Butterfly* story to Vietnam where Cio-Cio-San becomes Kim, a Vietnamese woman who becomes the mother of a child fathered by an American soldier who later abandons her. In 1988, David Henry Hwang wrote the play *M. Butterfly,* where in an unusual twist of the underlying story, Cio-Cio-San becomes Liling Song: a man.

Puccini's masterpiece received an unfavorable reception. In fact, the La Scala premiere was anticipated to be such a fiasco that Puccini was led to comment that he would be facing a lynch mob and a "Dantean inferno." Much of the legendary fiasco is attributed to jealousies and rivalries among his contemporaries; Puccini's publisher, Ricordi, was always providing his pet composer with the best librettos and librettists.

In addition, and aside from the fact that he was accused of plagiarizing his own *La Bohème,* it was the length of his second act which his public was unable to cope with. Later revisions by Puccini, including the addition of the third act tenor aria, solidified *Madama Butterfly* as one of the greatest operas in the Puccini canon, if not the entire operatic canon.

Butterfly seduces us as she seduced Pinkerton, and of course, seduced Puccini. Throughout Puccini's entire life, Butterfly remained his favorite heroine, unconsciously identifying, as we do, with the transformation and destruction of a soul, and the futile despair and terrible injuries that could be inflicted on a ravished innocent.

Principal Characters in the Opera

Cio-Cio-San (Madama Butterfly)	Soprano
Suzuki, her maid	Soprano
Pinkerton, Lieutenant in the U.S. Navy	Tenor
Sharpless, United States Consul	Baritone
Goro, a marriage broker	Tenor
Prince Yamadori, a Japanese suitor	Tenor
The Bonze, an uncle and priest	Bass
Imperial Commissioner	Bass
Official Registrar	Bass
Cio-Cio-San's mother	Soprano
An Aunt	Soprano
A Cousin	Soprano
Yakasude, an uncle	Tenor
Kate Pinkerton	Soprano

Dolore ("Trouble") Cio-Cio-San's child,
relations, friends, servants

TIME: Beginning of the 20th century

PLACE: Nagasaki, Japan

Brief Story Synopsis

The *Madama Butterfly* story juxtaposes a cultural collision between West and East, begging the question whether two distinctly different cultures can possibly unite in harmony.

The drama starts like a fairy tale, but ends in tragic disaster. Cio-Cio-San — Madama Butterfly — is a young Japanese ex-geisha, who fulfills her wish fantasy by marrying an American naval lieutenant, Benjamin Franklin Pinkerton. Yielding totally to her new husband, Butterfly abandons her ancient religion and converts to Christianity, an act which results in her becoming renounced and ostracized by her family.

After their wedding, Pinkerton abandons Butterfly, eventually marrying an American wife. Pinkerton and Butterfly have a child, but ultimately, Pinkerton and his new wife return to take the child from Butterfly. Butterfly's only recourse to save her honor is through ritual suicide, the noble death of hara kiri.

Butterfly's shifting emotions and thoughts make Puccini's opera a profound psychological music-drama; it poignantly portrays the pathos of the heroine's heart-wrenching decline and her state of mind as the dilemma of each crisis unfolds.

Butterfly becomes a genuine tragic figure as she develops from childlike innocence to adult understanding. She bravely faces her conflicts and destiny, butHer true heroic stature occurs when she accepts the pathetic reality that she must give up her child.

Story Narrative with Music Highlights

ACT I: Nagasaki, a house overlooking the harbor

There is bustling activity as Goro, a marriage broker and real-estate agent, leads Lieutenant Pinkerton about the house and demonstrates its various fragile appurtenances. Goro presents the domestic staff to Pinkerton: a cook, a servant, and his future wife's maid, Suzuki. Pinkerton becomes bored with their respectful chatter.

After Goro reels off the list of wedding guests, the American Consul Sharpless arrives. At Goro's bidding, servants bring drinks for Sharpless and his host. Pinkerton explains to the Consul that he has secured the house — and his new bride — according to Japanese fashion: a 999-year lease which he may terminate at a month's notice.

In his character exposition, "Dovunque al mondo," musically framed by the opening strains of "The Star Spangled Banner," Pinkerton outlines his easygoing philosophy: that of the roving "Yankee" who takes his pleasure where he finds it.

"Dovunque al mondo"

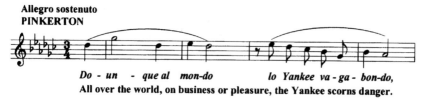

Allegro sostenuto
PINKERTON

Do - un - que al mon-do   lo Yankee va - ga - bon-do,
All over the world, on business or pleasure, the Yankee scorns danger.

Pinkerton tells Sharpless about Butterfly's charms and his infatuation with her. Sharpless recollects having seen her when she visited the consulate; her simple sincerity touched him deeply, and he hopes that Pinkerton will never break her heart. Pinkerton scoffs at his scruples, contemptuously damning him as a typical, unadventurous middle-aged man. Both drink a toast to America, and Pinkerton adds, to the day when he will consummate a real marriage: to a real American wife.

In the distance, female voices are heard, and Goro announces the arrival of Butterfly and her friends and family. Butterfly's entrance is magical, a dramatic and ironic transition that contrasts with Pinkerton's insensitive revelations.

Butterfly climbs the hill with her wedding entourage, and her words revel in this glorious wedding day in which her forthcoming marriage to Pinkerton will transform her, as she says, into "the happiest girl in all Japan and all the world," because she has "arrived to answer the call of love."

Butterfly's entrance music — the "Happiness motive" — is elegant, simple, and pulsating, a simple four-note phrase that ascends and rises chromatically, climaxing in a magnificently arching, lush, and sensuous musical finale. The "Happiness Motive" is the signature music of the opera, a leitmotif identifying Butterfly's bliss; Puccini later integrates the theme into the "Love Duet" ending Act 1, and into

Butterfly's triumphant exultation in Act II, when she believes that Pinkerton has returned. But the theme is also heard in musical variations and transformations that capture various states of mind, most emphatically, the abandoned Butterfly's expressions of nostalgia for her past happiness.

Butterfly's Entrance: "Happiness Motive"

Butterfly arrives and bows to the two men. Sharpless questions her about her background, and learns that her people were once wealthy, but have since fallen on hard times: the reason that she has earned her living as a geisha. Butterfly is 15 years old, and the astonished Sharpless again repeats his warning to Pinkerton. More guests arrive, including Butterfly's mother, a Cousin, an Aunt, and Uncle Yakuside, whose immediate concern is wine and refreshment. Meanwhile, the women exchange impressions of the bridegroom — not all of them favorable — and some express jealousy and envy, At a signal from Butterfly, they all bow to Pinkerton, and then disperse.

Alone, Butterfly shows Pinkerton her treasures and mementos which she keeps concealed in her voluminous sleeves — a clasp, a clay pipe, a girdle, a pot of rouge, and a narrow sheath about which she hesitates further discussion. Goro intervenes and explains that the sheath holds the dagger with which Butterfly's father committed hara kiri at the emperor's command. Butterfly produces puppets that represent the spirits of her ancestors.

However, Butterfly's love for Pinkerton is total. She tells Pinkerton — making sure that her relations cannot hear her — that she visited the American mission to renounce her ancestral religion and embrace that of her husband: Christianity.

Conversion aria:

Goro calls for silence. The Imperial Commissioner very quickly performs the wedding ceremony, and afterwards, all join in a toast to the couple's happiness.

The wedding festivities are interrupted by Butterfly's uncle, the Bonze (a Buddhist priest), who has learned of Butterfly's conversion to Christianity. He denounces her for having forsworn her faith, and the relatives likewise renounce Butterfly. In a frenzy of shouting against Butterfly, all depart.

Renunciation Motive:

As evening falls, Pinkerton comforts Butterfly, who is in tears and trembling after being renounced and ostracized by her family and friends.

Love Duet: "Viene la sera"

Butterfly and Pinkerton rejoice in their overflowing love. Two musical themes alternate and collide: the theme underscoring the Bonze's renunciation of Butterfly, with triumphant renderings of her "Happiness Motive": fear and happiness are the haunting ironies of this blissful moment.

Butterfly fears to speak of her love for Pinkerton, but Pinkerton assures her of the life-giving vitality of love. The "Love Duet" becomes an ecstatic moment of operatic bliss.

"È Notte Serena"

The final chords of the duet are dissonant and tonically unresolved; Puccini's music tells us that this blissful appearance of consummated love is not resolved.

Act II: The interior of Butterfly's house

Three years have gone by. Pinkerton sailed away after the wedding and has not been heard from since. Butterfly is alone with Suzuki, the latter praying to the Japanese gods to end her mistress's sufferings. Butterfly retorts that such gods are lazy; Pinkerton's god would soon come to her aid if only he knew where to find her. Their funds are nearly exhausted, and Suzuki expresses doubts whether Pinkerton will ever return, reminding Butterfly that foreign husbands never return after they have departed. Furious, Butterfly reminds her how Pinkerton had arranged for the consul to pay the rent, how he had put locks on the doors to protect her from her family, and how he had promised to return "when the robins build their nests."

Butterfly becomes inspired with a vision, her imagination anticipating Pinkerton's return. In the aria "Un bel di" ("One beautiful day"), she fantasizes a scenario in which she describes her joy and ecstasy as she watches Pinkerton returning, a little speck from afar climbing the hill.

The "Un bel di" affirms Butterfly's faith, as well as her despair.

"Un bel di"

Andante molto calmo
BUTTERFLY

Un   bel di ve - dre-mo   le var   - si un fil di fu - mo,
One beautiful day, we will see a thread of smoke arising on the sea..

Goro arrives with Sharpless, who had not seen Butterfly since the wedding three years ago. Sharpless brings a letter from Pinkerton. Butterfly cordially welcomes him, and immediately inquires how often the robins build their nests in America. Sharpless is evasive, but duly astonished by her naivete.

The wealthy Prince Yamadori arrives and pursues his offer of marriage to Butterfly. She mockingly rejects him, proudly announcing that she is a married woman according to the laws of America, where divorce, she says, is a punishable offense. Yamadori departs in frustration, confused and perplexed that he has been spurned and rejected by Butterfly.

Sharpless begins to read Pinkerton's letter, but becomes frustrated by Butterfly's childish interruptions. Each time he starts reading, Butterfly hears only what she wants to hear, interrupting him with her own interpretation of its content, and believing that the letter is an announcement that her husband will soon return.

Sharpless tries to tell Butterfly that Pinkerton intends to go out of Butterfly's life forever, but she misunderstands the letter's drift, and in frustration, Sharpless abandons the task.

Sharpless angers Butterfly by suggesting that she accept Yamadori's offer. Butterfly becomes enraged, and hurries to fetch her son. Addressing herself to her son, she reveals that if she were to resume the horrible profession of becoming a geisha again, she would rather die by her own hand.

"Che tua madre"

Andante molto mosso
BUTTERFLY

Che   tua   ma -   dre   do - vrà pren-der - ti in brac - cio,
That your mother should take you in her arms...

Sharpless leaves, but is profoundly moved by Butterfly's fate. He promises Butterfly that he will inform Pinkerton of their son.

Suzuki drags in Goro, whom she accuses of spreading slanderous rumors. Butterfly threatens to kill him, but then dismisses him with contempt.

A loud cannon shot is heard from the harbor, the traditional announcement of the arrival of an American warship. The background music reechoes the aria "Un bel di," Butterfly's fantasy about Pinkerton's return. Butterfly takes a telescope in hand and trembles with excitement as she identifies the flag and colors of the warship Abraham Lincoln, Pinkerton's ship.

For Butterfly, the agony of waiting has ended. In exultation – to the musical themes of the "Happiness motive," "Love Duet," and the "Star Spangled Banner" — Butterfly explodes in triumph. Pinkerton has indeed returned, confirming that their love is secure and eternal. She was right all the time, and she now expresses her contempt and disdain for being renounced by her people and relatives, her scorn at the presumptive and arrogant Yamadori, and Goro's scandalous lies.

Butterfly has arrived at her triumphal moment of victory. Everyone told her that all hope had vanished, but her love and faith have prevailed. Butterfly has been vindicated because Pinkerton is returning.

Butterfly and Suzuki celebrate this euphoric and ecstatic moment, an event she has anticipated for 3 years. They adorn the house with flowers so that Pinkerton will see "springtime glory." After all, as Butterfly comments, it was her devotion and tears that made those flowers grow.

Butterfly and Suzuki: "Flower Duet"

Allegretto moderato
BUTTERFLY and SUZUKI

Ge - tia - mo a ma - ni   pie - ne   mammole e tu - be - ro - se,
We throw handfuls of violets and white roses,

As the sun begins to set, Butterfly dresses herself in her wedding obi, so that she may greet Pinkerton as he remembered her in their last moments of happiness on their wedding day three years earlier. Butterfly looks into a mirror, and laments how time and her longing have changed her; her smile is now saddened, and she has aged.

Together with the child and Suzuki, Butterfly maintains a vigil throughout the night. She punches three little holes in the soshi screen so they can watch for Pinkerton. Suzuki, Butterfly, and the boy, all rigid, statuesque, and motionless, settle down for their night vigil, poised as they face the harbor. The boy and Suzuki fall asleep, but Butterfly remains awake throughout the night.

The orchestra ironically repeats the musical themes from the "Letter Scene:" the music seemingly a lullaby, but it is injected with ominous appearances and variations of the "Renunciation Motive," further emphasizing Butterfly's pathetic futility, utter isolation, and ominous fate. The "Night Vigil" — night becoming day — provides a host of musical imagery as day dawns, birds chirp, and there are sounds of morning activity in the harbor.

ACT III: Butterfly's house

Pinkerton has been told by Sharpless that he has fathered a child. Act III deals with Pinkerton, his new American wife, Kate, and their determination to rescue the child from the perceived squalor of Japanese life; their intention is to bring the child to America.

The sun rises to reveal Butterfly, Suzuki and the child seated in their overnight vigil of waiting. Butterfly sings a lullaby, and then takes the boy to another room where she quickly falls asleep.

Pinkerton and Sharpless arrive. Suzuki catches sight of a woman in the garden, and is informed by Sharpless that she is Pinkerton's wife, Kate. Their concern, he tells her, is to rescue the child and ensure that he receives a good American upbringing.

Sharpless reproaches Pinkerton for his heartlessness. Pinkerton's return becomes a traumatic moment of revelation for him. He reflects on the bitterness of the flowers, which he perceives as symbols of faded love. He senses death filling the air. Pinkerton has awakened to recognize his callousness and selfishness and begs forgiveness. Now overcome with emotion, he cannot bear his own guilt any longer and admits his remorse. Sharpless reminds him that he prophesied this tragedy, but Pinkerton was deaf and unheeding to his warnings.

Pinkerton's aria, "Addio fiorito asil" ("Farewell, sanctuary of flowers and home of love"), is a stunning operatic moment of introspection and transformation; Pinkerton realizes his grave and fatal errors, and concludes that peace will never return to him; he will always be haunted and tormented by guilt. Pinkerton leaves abruptly, unable to face the woman he has betrayed.

"Addio fiorito asil"

Butterfly awakens and confronts Sharpless, Suzuki, and Kate. When she is made aware of their wishes, she decides to obey with noble dignity. She bids them retire; Pinkerton himself should come for the child in half an hour.

While Suzuki's sobs are heard in the background, Butterfly kneels before the Buddha. In conclusive moves, Butterfly removes her father's dagger from the shrine, kisses the blade, and reads its inscription:

"Con onor muore chi non puo serbar vita con onore."
("One shall die with honor who no longer can live his life with honor.")

Suzuki pushes the child to his mother. Butterfly sings a poignant farewell to him, urging him to look into her face and remember her features; the loving mother who was forced to abandon her adored child.

Butterfly's farewell:

Butterfly sends the boy out, and then goes behind the screen where she fatally stabs herself with the dagger.

Pinkerton is heard anxiously calling: *Butterfly, Butterfly, Butterfly.*

Butterfly falls, and dies.

MADAMA BUTTERFLY

Libretto

ACT I

A Japanese house with a terrace that overlooks the harbor and town of Nagasaki.
Goro shows Pinkerton details of the house he has rented.

Pinkerton
E soffitto, e pareti.

Pinkerton
And the walls and the ceiling.

Goro
Vanno e vengono a prova a norma che vi
giova nello stesso locale alternar nuovi
aspetti ai consueti.

Goro
They move in and out to suit your fancy,
varying the interior and the exterior in the
same surroundings.

Pinkerton
Il nido nuzïal dov'è?

Pinkerton
Where is the marriage chamber?

Goro
Qui, o là, secondo.

Goro
Here, or there, according to your whims.

Pinkerton
Anch'esso a doppio fondo!
La sala?

Pinkerton
A wonderful contrivance!
The hall?

Goro
Ecco!

Goro *(showing the terrace)*
There!

Pinkerton
All'aperto?

Pinkerton *(displaying amazement)*
In the open?

Goro
Un fianco scorre.

Goro *(sliding the partitions)*
A wall slides outward.

Pinkerton
Capisco! Capisco! Un altro.

Pinkerton
I see now! I see it! Another.

Goro
Scivola!

Goro
It slides!

Pinkerton
E la dimora frivola.

Pinkerton
It is a fairy-tale dwelling.

Goro
Salda come una torre da terra, fino al
tetto.

Goro
It rises like a tower from base to attic.

Pinkerton
È una casa a soffietto.

Pinkerton
It comes and goes as if by magic!

Goro claps his hands. Two men and a woman appear and kneel before Pinkerton.

Goro
Questa è la cameriera che della vostra
sposa fu già serva amorosa.
Il cuoco, il servitor. Son confusi del
grande onore.

Goro
This is the maid who has served your wife
lovingly.
The cook, the servant. They're embarrassed by such a great honor.

Pinkerton
I nomi?

Pinkerton
Their names?

Goro
Miss Nuvola Leggera.
Raggio di Sol Nascente.
Esala Aromi.

Goro
Miss Gentle Breeze-of-Morning.
Ray-of-the-Rising-Sun.
Aromatic-Pinetree.

Suzuki
Sorride Vostro Onore?
Il riso è frutto e fiore.
Disse il savio Ocunama:
dei crucci la trama smaglia il sorriso.

Suzuki
Your Honor wishes a smile?
The smile is as fair as flowers.
Thus spake the wise Ocunama:
a smile conquers all and defies all troubles.

Schiude alla perla il guscio,
apre all'uomo l'uscio del Paradiso,
profumo degli Dei, fontana della vita.
Disse il savio Ocunama:
dei crucci la trama smaglia il sorriso.

Pearls may be won by smiling,
but smiles can open the portals of Paradise,
the perfume of the Gods, and the fountain
of life. Thus spake the wise Ocunama: A
smile conquers all and defies all troubles.

Goro notices that Pinkerton seems bored so he dismisses the three servants.

Pinkerton
A chiacchiere costei mi par cosmopolita.

Che guardi?

Pinkerton
They babble just like all women.
(Goro looks toward Nagasaki)
What are you looking at?

Goro
Se non giunge ancor la sposa.

Goro
To see if the bride is arriving yet.

Pinkerton
Tutto è pronto?

Pinkerton
Is everything ready?

Goro
Ogni cosa.

Goro *(bowing accomodatingly)*
Every detail.

Pinkerton
Gran perla di sensale!

Goro
Qui verran: l'Ufficiale del registro, i
parenti, il vostro Console,
la fidanzata. Qui si firma l'atto
e il matrimonio è fatto.

Pinkerton
E son molti i parenti?

Goro
La suocera, la nonna, lo zio Bonzo
(che non ci degnerà di sua presenza)
e cugini, e le cugine.
Mettiam fra gli ascendenti
ed i collaterali, un due dozzine.
Quanto alla discendenza provvederanno
assai Vostra Grazia e la bella Butterfly.

Pinkerton
Gran perla di sensale!

Sharpless
E suda e arrampica!
Sbuffa, inciampica!

Goro
Il Consol sale.

Sharpless
Ah! Quei ciottoli mi hanno sfiaccato!

Pinkerton
Bene arrivato.

Goro
Bene arrivato.

Sharpless
Ouff!

Pinkerton
Presto Goro qualche ristoro.

Pinkerton
You're a superb broker!

Goro
The official registrar will come here, the
relations, your country's Consul,
your future wife. Here you'll sign the
contract and then the marriage is complete.

Pinkerton
Are there many relations?

Goro
Her mother, grandmother, and the uncle
Bonze (he'll not honor us with his
appearance) and male and female cousins.
Of ancestors and other blood relations,
around two dozen. As to the descendants,
I reckon that Your Honor and the lovely
Butterfly can figure that out.

Pinkerton
You're a superb broker!

Sharpless *(from the distance)*
A plague on this steep ascent!
I'm winded and stumbling!

Goro
Here comes the Consul.

Sharpless
Ah! The scramble up has left me breathless!

Pinkerton
Welcome.

Goro
Welcome.

Sharpless
Ough!

Pinkerton
Quickly Goro, some refreshments.

Sharpless
Alto.

Sharpless *(panting as he looks around)*
Quite a view!

Pinkerton
Ma bello!

Pinkerton *(pointing to the view]*
But lovely!

Sharpless
Nagasaki, il mare, il porto.

Sharpless
Nagasaki, the ocean, the harbor.

Pinkerton
E una casetta che obbedisce a bacchetta.

Pinkerton
It is a house that obeys a magic wand.

*Goro returns from the house with two servants who bring
glasses, bottles, a small table, and two chairs.*

Sharpless
Vostra?

Sharpless *(referring to the house)*
Yours?

Pinkerton
La comperai per novecentonovantanove
anni, con facoltà, ogni mese, di rescindere
i patti.
Sono in questo paese elastici del par, case
e contratti.

Pinkerton
I bought this house for nine hundred and
ninety-nine years, but with the option to
cancel the contract every month.
In this country the houses and the
contracts are elastic!

Sharpless
E l'uomo esperto ne profitta.

Sharpless
An expert can profit from it.

Pinkerton
Certo.

Pinkerton
Surely.

Allegro sostenuto
PINKERTON

Do - un - que al mon-do   *lo Yankee va - ga - bon-do,*

Pinkerton
Dovunque al mondo lo Yankee
vagabondo
si gode e traffica sprezzando rischi.
Affonda l'áncora alla ventura.

Milk-Punch, o Wisky?

Pinkerton
All over the world, on business or
pleasure, the Yankee scorns danger.
His lays anchor for adventure.

(Pinkerton interrupts himself)
Milk-Punch, or Whisky?

Affonda l'áncora alla ventura finchè una
raffica scompigli nave e ormeggi, alberatura.
La vita ei non appaga se non fa suo tesor
i fiori d'ogni plaga.

He lays anchor for adventure until a
squall upsets his ship, sails and rigging.
And life is not worth living if he can't
win the best and fairest of each country.

Sharpless
È un facile vangelo.

Sharpless
That's an easygoing gospel.

Pinkerton
...d'ogni bella gli amor.

Pinkerton
...and the beauty of love.

Sharpless
È un facile vangelo che fa la vita vaga
ma che intristisce il cor.

Sharpless
A very easy gospel that can make life
pleasant, but fatal to another.

Pinkerton
Vinto si tuffa, la sorte racciuffa.
Il suo talento fa in ogni dove.
Così mi sposo all'uso giapponese
per novecento novantanove anni.
Salvo a prosciogliermi ogni mese.

Pinkerton
He is undaunted, and fate cannot crush
him. His talent always succeeds.
And so I'm marrying in Japanese
fashion for nine hundred and ninety-nine
years, free to annul the marriage monthly.

Sharpless
È un facile vangelo.

Sharpless
An easy going gospel.

Pinkerton
"America forever!"

Pinkerton (*toasts with Sharpless*)
"America forever!"

Sharpless
"America forever!"

Sharpless
"America forever!"

Sharpless
Ed è bella la sposa?

Sharpless
Is the bride very pretty?

Goro
Una ghirlanda di fiori freschi.
Una stella dai raggi d'oro.
E per nulla: sol cento yen.

Se Vostra Grazia mi comanda ce n'ho un
assortimento.

Goro (*interrupting*)
Fair as a garland of fragrant flowers.
Brighter than a star in the heavens.
And for nothing: one hundred yen.
(*to the Consul*)
If Your Honor entrusts me, I have a fine
selection.
(*The Consul laughingly declines.*)

Pinkerton
Va, conducila Goro.

Pinkerton (*impatiently*)
Go and fetch her, Goro.

Sharpless
Quale smania vi prende!
Sareste addirittura còtto?

Pinkerton
Non so! Non so!
Dipende dal grado di cottura!
Amore o grillo, dir non saprei.
Certo costei m'ha coll'ingenue arti
invescato.
Lieve qual tenue vetro soffiato alla
statura, al portamento sembra figura da
paravento.
Ma dal suo lucido fondo di lacca come
con subito moto si stacca,
qual farfalletta svolazza e posa
con tal grazietta silenzïosa,
che di rincorrerla furor m'assale
se pure infrangerne dovessi l'ale.

Sharpless
Ier l'altro, il Consolato sen' venne a
visitar!
Io non la vidi, ma l'udii parlar.
Di sua voce il mistero l'anima mi colpì.
Certo quando è sincer l'amor parla così.
Sarebbe gran peccato le lievi ali strappar
e desolar forse un credulo cuor.

Pinkerton
Console mio garbato, quetatevi! Si sa.

Sharpless
Sarebbe gran peccato.

Pinkerton
la vostra età è di flebile umor.
Non c'è gran male s'io vo' quell'ale
drizzare ai dolci voli dell'amor!

Sharpless
Quella divina mite vocina non dovrebbe
dar note di dolor!

Pinkerton
Wisky?

Sharpless
What folly has seized you!
Are you intoxicated?

Pinkerton
I don't know! I don't know!
It depends what you call intoxication!
I cannot tell you if it is love or fancy.
All I know is that her innocent charm has
entranced me.
She delights me. She's fragile and
slender, dainty in stature,
and a quaint little figure.
She seems like a figure from a painted
screen or from a work of lacquer. She's
light as a feather and flutters like a
butterfly, hovering and settling with
gracious silence. I want to run after her
furiously and break her fragile wings.

Sharpless
The other day, she came to the Consulate!
I did not see her, but I heard her speak.
Her mysterious voice touched my very
soul.
Surely, her love for you speaks sincerely.
It would be sad and pitiful to break those
dainty wings and torment a trusting heart.

Pinkerton
Dear Consul, allay your fears! One knows.

Sharpless
It would be sad and pitiful.

Pinkerton
Men of your age look on life gloomily.
It is no great sin if I guide those wings to
tender flights of love!

Sharpless
No cry of anguish should ever be uttered
by that gentle and trusting little soul!

Pinkerton
Whisky?

Sharpless
Un'altro bicchiere.

Sharpless
Yes, another glass.

Sharpless
Bevo alla vostra famiglia lontana.

Sharpless *(toasting)*
I drink to your family far away.

Pinkerton
E al giorno in cui mi sposerò con vere
nozze a una vera sposa americana.

Pinkerton
And to the day of my real marriage to a
real American wife.

Goro
Ecco! Son giunte al sommo del pendìo.
Già del femmmineo sciame qual di vento
in fogliame s'ode il brusìo.

Goro *(reappearing and breathless)*
See them! They've arrived at the hill!
A crowd of women bustling like rustling
branches in the wind.

Le Amiche di Butterfly
Ah! Ah! Ah!
Quanto cielo! quanto mar!
Quanto cielo! quanto mar!

Butterfly's Friends *(from the distance)*
Ah! Ah! Ah!
So much sky! So much sea!
So much sky! So much sea!

Butterfly
Ancora un passo or via.

Butterfly
One step more to climb.

Le Amiche
Come sei tarda!

Girl Friends
You'll be late!

Butterfly
Aspetta.

Butterfly
One moment.

Le Amiche
Ecco la vetta.
Guarda, guarda quanti fior!

Girl Friends
Here is the summit.
Look, look, so many flowers!

Largo
BUTTERFLY

Spi - ra sul ma - re e sul - la ter - ra,

Butterfly
Spira sul mare e sulla terra.

Butterfly
Across the sea and over the land.

Le Amiche
Quanto cielo! Quanto mar!

Girl Friends
So much sky! So much sea!

Butterfly
Un primaveril soffio giocondo.

Butterfly
A balmy spring breeze blows.

Sharpless
O allegro cinguettar di gioventù!

Sharpless
Oh happy youthful chirping!

Butterfly
Io sono la fanciulla più lieta del
Giappone, anzi del mondo.
Amiche, io son venuta al richiamo d'amor
d'amor venni alle soglie.

Butterfly
I am the happiest girl in Japan, and in all
the world!
Friends, I have arrived to answer the call
of love; love has arrived where I stand.

Le Amiche
Quanti fior! Quanto mar!
Gioia a te, gioia a te sia dolce amica.

Girl Friends
So many flowers! So much sea!
Joy to you, joy to our gentle friend!

Butterfly
Ove s'accoglie il bene di chi vive e di chi
muor.

Butterfly
Here is the glory where life or death
awaits me.

Le Amiche
Ma pria di varcar la soglia che t'attira
volgiti e mira.
Volgiti e mira le cose che ti son care,
mira quanto cielo, quanti fiori, quanto mar!

Girl Friends
But look beyond the threshold and admire
the panorama.
Turn and admire the things you hold so dear;
admire how much sky, flowers and sea!

Butterfly
Amiche, io son venuta al richiamo
d'amor,
al richiamo d'amor,
son venuta al richiamo d'amor!

Butterfly
My friends, I have answered the call of
love,
and the call of my heart.
I have come to answer the call of love!

Le Amiche
Gioia a te, gioia a te sia dolce amica,
ma pria di varcar la soglia volgiti indietro
e mira,
le cose tutte che ti son sì care!

Girl Friends
Joy to you, joy to you gentle friend,
but look beyond the threshold and admire
the panorama,
the things you hold so dear!

Butterfly
Siam giunte.
F. B. Pinkerton. Giù.

Butterfly
We've arrived.
B. F. Pinkerton. Down.

Le Amiche
Giù.

Girl Friends (all kneel)
Down.

Butterfly
Gran ventura.

Butterfly
August sir.

Le Amiche
Riverenza.

Girl Friends
Most revered one.

Pinkerton
È un po' dura la scalata?

Pinkerton *(smiling)*
The ascent was difficult?

Butterfly
A una sposa costumata più penosa è
l'impazienza.

Butterfly
Not so trying as were those weary hours
of waiting.

Pinkerton
Molto raro complimento!

Pinkerton
What a rare compliment!

Butterfly
Dei più belli ancor ne so.

Butterfly
I know better ones than that.

Pinkerton
Dei gioielli!

Pinkerton
Gems, no doubt!

Butterfly
Se vi è caro sul momento...

Butterfly
If you care for some right now...

Pinkerton
Grazie, no.

Pinkerton
Thank you, no.

Sharpless
"Miss Butterfly"
Bel nome, vi sta a meraviglia.
Siete di Nagasaki?

Sharpless
Miss "Butterfly."
Your name is so marvelous.
Are you from Nagasaki?

Butterfly
Signor sì. Di famiglia assai prospera un
tempo.
Verità?

Butterfly
Sir, I am. My family was formerly
wealthy. *(turning to her friends)*
Is it true?

Le Amiche
Verità!

Girl Friends
It is true!

Butterfly
Nessuno si confessa mai nato in povertà,
non c'è vagabondo che a sentirlo non sia
di gran prosapia. Eppur conobbi la
ricchezza. Ma il turbine rovescia le
quercie più robuste, e abbiam fatto la
ghescia per sostentarci.
Vero?

Butterfly
No one confesses that he was born in
poverty; there isn't a vagrant who won't
tell you of his ancient lineage. And yet I
have indeed known riches. But the storm
made the strongest oak fall, and we had to
become geishas to survive. *(to her friends)*
True?

Le Amiche
Vero!

Girl Friends
True!

Butterfly
Non lo nascondo, nè m'adonto.

Ridete? Perché?
Cose del mondo.

Butterfly
I don't hide it, and don't blush because of
it. (noticing that Sharpless smiles)
You're laughing? Why?
That's the way of the world.

Pinkerton
(Con quel fare di bambola quando parla
m'infiamma.)

Pinkerton (to Sharpless)
(With her innocent baby-face, when she
speaks she sets my heart aflame.)

Sharpless
E ci avete sorelle?

Sharpless (continues to question her)
Do you have any sisters?

Butterfly
Non signore. Ho la mamma.

Butterfly
None, Sir. I have my mother.

Goro
Una nobile dama.

Goro
A most noble lady.

Butterfly
Ma senza farle torto povera molto
anch'essa.

Butterfly
But it is not her fault that she is so
dreadfully poor.

Sharpless
E vostro padre?

Sharpless
And your father?

Butterfly
Morto.

Butterfly (tersely)
Dead.

Sharpless
Quant' anni avete?

Sharpless
How old are you?

Butterfly
Indovinate.

Butterfly (childishly)
Now try to guess it!

Sharpless
Dieci.

Sharpless
Ten years.

Butterfly
Crescete.

Butterfly
Guess higher.

Sharpless
Venti.

Sharpless
Twenty.

Butterfly
Calate.
Quindici netti, netti;
sono vecchia diggià.

Butterfly
Guess lower.
Fifteen, exactly, fifteen!
I am old, am I not?

Sharpless
Quindici anni!

Sharpless
Fifteen years old!

Pinkerton
Quindici anni!

Pinkerton
Fifteen years old!

Sharpless
L'età dei giuochi.

Sharpless
The age of playthings.

Pinkerton
E dei confetti.

Pinkerton
And of sweet foods!

Goro
L'Imperial Commissario, l'Ufficiale
del registro, i congiunti.

Goro *(Goro announces new arrivals)*
The august Imperial Commissioner; the
Official Registrar; the relations.

Pinkerton
Fate presto.

Pinkerton *(to Goro)*
Hurry up now.

*Butterfly's relations arrive. Pinkerton takes Sharpless to the side and
laughingly looks at the quaint group of relations.*

Pinkerton
Che burletta la sfilata della nova
parentela, tolta in prestito, a mesata!

Pinkerton
This procession of my new relations is a
farce, held on terms of monthly contract!

Parenti ed Amiche
Dov'è?

Relations and friends *(to Butterfly)*
Where is he?

Butterfly, Parenti ed Amiche
Eccolo là!

Butterfly, Relations and friends
There he is!

Una Cugina, Parenti ed Amici
Bello non è.

A Cousin, Relations and friends
He's not so handsome.

Pinkerton
Certo dietro a quella vela
di ventaglio pavonazzo,
la mia suocera si cela.

Pinkerton *(observing the women)*
I'm certain that there behind that
gigantic fan of peacock feathers,
my mother-in-law is hiding.

Parenti ed Amiche
Mi pare un re!

Relations and friends
He seems like a king!

La Madre
Mi pare un re!

The Mother *(with deep admiration)*
He seems like a king!

La Cugina
Goro l'offrì pur anco a me, ma s'ebbe un no!

Cousin *(to Butterfly)*
Goro offered him to me first, but I said no!

Butterfly
Si, giusto tu!

Butterfly *(contemptuously to her Cousin)*
A likely story!

Pinkerton
E quel coso da strapazzo è lo zio briaco e pazzo.

Pinkerton *(pointing to Yakuside)*
And that shabby looking fool is the mad drunken uncle.

Parenti, Amici ed Amiche
Ecco, perché prescelta fu, vuol far con te la soprappiù.

Relations and friends
You will agree that if that is true, that's why she looks down on you.

Parenti ed Amiche
La sua beltà già disfiorì.

Relations and friends
I think her beauty's fading.

Parenti, Amici ed Amiche
Divorzierà.

Relations and friends
He'll divorce her.

Cugina, Parenti ed Amiche
Spero di sì.

Cousin, Relations and friends
I hope he won't.

Goro
Per carità tacete un po'.

Goro *(annoyed at the idle chatter)*
For goodness sake be quiet!

Lo Zio Yakuside
Vino ce n'è?

Uncle Yakuside
Is there wine?

La Madre, la Zia
Guardiamo un po'.

The Mother the Aunt
Let's look around.

Parenti ed Amiche
Ne vidi già color di thè, color di thè e chermisì!

Relations and friends
I've just seen some, the color of tea, the color of tea and crimson too!

La sua beltà già disfiorì, già disfiorì.
Divorzierà.

I think her beauty's fading.
yes, fading. He'll divorce her.

Zio Yakuside
Vino ce n'è? Guardiamo un po',
guardiamo un po'.
Ne vidi già color di thè, e chermisi, color
di thè.
Vino ce n'è? Vediamo un po'!

Uncle Yakuside
Is there no wine? Let's look around, let's
look around.
I've just seen some the color of tea, and
crimson too.
Is there no wine? Let's look around!

Goro
Per carità tacete un po'!
Sch! Sch! Sch!

Goro
For pity's sake be silent now!
Sh! Sh! Sh!

Sharpless
O amico fortunato!

Sharpless *(aside to Pinkerton)*
Oh fortunate friend!

Pinkerton
Sì, è vero, è un fiore, un fiore!

Pinkerton
Yes, it's true, she's a flower!

Sharpless
O fortunato Pinkerton!

Sharpless
Oh fortunate friend!

Pinkerton
L'esotico suo odore

Pinkerton
The aroma is exotic.

Sharpless
Che in sorte v'è toccato

Sharpless
What fate has touched you.

Pinkerton
M'ha il cervello sconvolto.

Pinkerton
She fans the flames of my passion.

Sharpless
Un fior pur or sbocciato!
Non più bella e d'assai fanciulla io vidi
mai di questa Butterfly.
E se a voi sembran scede
il patto e la sua fede.

Sharpless
A flower that has hardly opened!
I have never seen such a beautiful girl as
this Butterfly.
Don't make a folly of this contract
and on faith.

Parenti ed Amiche e la Cugina
Senza tanto ricercar io ne trovo dei
miglior, e gli dirò un bel no, e gli dirò di
no, di no!

Relations and Friends
One could search far and wide and not find
a better man, To find a better men than him,
is impossible, I would answer no, no, no!

Parenti ed Amiche e la Madre
No, mia cara, non mi par, è davvero un
gran signor, nè gli direi di no,
nè mai direi di no, di no!

Relations and Friends and Mother
No, my dear, that is not so, He's truly a
great man, I'd never answer no,
I'd never answer no, no, no!

Butterfly
Badate, attenti a me.

Pinkerton
Sì, è vero, è un fiore, un fiore, e in fede
mia l'ho colto!

Sharpless
Badate! Ella ci crede.

Butterfly
Mamma, vien qua.

Badate a me:attenti, orsù, uno, due, tre e
tutti giù.

Butterfly *(to her people)*
Attention, if you please.

Pinkerton
Yes it's true, she's a flower that has
broken my will!

Sharpless
I warn you! She believes in you.

Butterfly *(to her mother)*
Mother, come here,
(to the others)
Listen to me: all of you look, one, two,
three, all of you down!

All kneel before Pinkerton and Sharpless.
Pinkerton takes Butterfly's hand and leads her towards the house.

Pinkerton
Vieni, amor mio!
Vi piace la casetta?

Butterfly
Signor B. F. Pinkerton,
perdono...Io vorrei... pochi oggetti
da donna.

Pinkerton
Dove sono?

Butterfly
Sono qui. Vi dispiace?

Pinkerton
O perché mai, mia bella Butterfly?

Butterfly
Fazzoletti. La pipa. Una cintura.
Un piccolo fermaglio.
Uno specchio. Un ventaglio.

Pinkerton
Quel barattolo?

Pinkerton
Come, my love!
Do you like the little house?

Butterfly
Mister B. F. Pinkerton,
forgive me...I should like to... a young
girl's few possessions.

Pinkerton
But where are they?

Butterfly *(pointing to her sleeves)*
They are here. Are you angry?

Pinkerton *(astonished)*
Oh why, my dear little Butterfly?

Butterfly *(empties her sleeves)*
Silken kerchiefs. A pipe. A ribbon.
A small silver buckle.
A mirror. A fan.

Pinkerton *(looking at a jar)*
What is that you have?

Butterfly
Un vaso di tintura.

Pinkerton
Ohibò!

Butterfly
Vi spiace?

Via!

Pinkerton
E quello?

Butterfly
Cosa sacra e mia.

Pinkerton
E non si può vedere?

Butterfly
C'è troppa gente.
Perdonate.

Goro
È un presente del Mikado a suo padre,
coll'invito.

Pinkerton
E suo padre?

Goro
Ha obbedito.

Butterfly
Gli Ottokè.

Pinkerton
Quei pupazzi? Avete detto?

Butterfly
Son l'anime degli avi.

Pinkerton
Ah! Il mio rispetto.

Butterfly
A jar of carmine.

Pinkerton
Eeks!

Butterfly
It displeases you?
(throws away the jar)
There!

(She unveils a long sheath)
Pinkerton
And that?

Butterfly *(very gravely)*
That is sacred to me.

Pinkerton *(curiously)*
And can I see it?

Butterfly
There are too many people here.
Pardon me.

Goro *(whispers to Pinkerton)*
It was sent by the Mikado to her father,
with an invitation.
(imitating the act of suicide)

Pinkerton *(whispering)*
And her father?

Goro
He was obedient.

Butterfly
The Ottokè.

Pinkerton
These small figures? Can you mean it?

Butterfly
They are the souls of my forefathers.

Pinkerton
Ah! My respect.

Butterfly
Ieri son salita tutta sola in secreto alla
Missione.
Colla nuova mia vita posso adottare
nuova religione.
Lo zio Bonzo nol sa, nè i miei lo sanno.

Butterfly *(confidentially to Pinkerton)*
Yesterday I went to the Mission alone and
secretly.
I went there to adopt a new religion for
my new life.
My uncle Bonzo or the others don't know it.

Andante
BUTTERFLY

Io   se - guo il mio de - sti - no   e pie - na   d'u - mil - tà,

Io seguo il mio destino e piena d'umiltà
al Dio del signor Pinkerton m'inchino.
È mio destino.
Nella stessa chiesetta in ginocchio con
voi
pregherò lo stesso Dio.
E per farvi contento potrò quasi obliar la
gente mia.
Amore mio!

I humbly follow my fate and will kneel
before Pinkerton's God.
It is my destiny.
I will kneel in the same church as you and
pray to the same God.
And to make you happy, I will forsake my
ancestral religion!
(throws away the images]
My love!

Butterfly cuts herself short, fearful that her relatives have overheard her.
Meanwhile Goro opens the shoshi to announce that all is ready
for the wedding to proceed.

Goro
Tutti zitti!

Goro
Silence, silence!

Pinkerton and Butterfly stand together before the Imperial Commissioner.

Commissario
È concesso al nominato
Mister B. F. Pinkerton,
Luogotenente nella cannoniera
Lincoln, marina degli Stati Uniti
America del Nord:
ed alla damigella Butterfly
del quartiere d'Omara-Nagasaki,
d'unirsi in matrimonio, per dritto
il primo, della propria volontà,
ed ella per consenso dei parenti
qui testimonî all'atto.

The Commissioner
A writ has been given to the undersigned,
Mister B. F. Pinkerton,
Lieutenant serving on the gunboat
Lincoln, ship of the United States Navy
of North America:
and to the maiden known as Butterfly,
inhabitant of Omara-Nagasaki,
to join in the bonds of wedlock. To wit
the former, of his free accord and will,
and the latter, with the consent of her
relations, all here witness their marriage.

Goro
Lo sposo.

Poi la sposa.

E tutto è fatto.

Goro *(ceremoniously)*
The bridegroom.
(Pinkerton signs)
Now the bride.
(Butterfly signs)
And all is settled.

Relatives sign, and then friends approach Butterfly, congratulating her with deep bows.

Le Amiche
Madama Butterfly.

Girl Friends
Madam Butterfly.

Butterfly
Madama B. F. Pinkerton.

Butterfly *(correcting them)*
Madam B. F. Pinkerton.

Commissario
Augurî molti.

The Commissioner *(to Pinkerton)*
The best of wishes.

Pinkerton
I miei ringraziamenti.

Pinkerton
My thanks.

Commissario
Il signor Console scende?

The Commissioner *(to Sharpless)*
Are you leaving?

Sharpless
L'accompagno.
Ci vedrem domani.

Sharpless
I'll go with you. *(to Pinkerton)*
We'll see each other tomorrow?

Pinkerton
A meraviglia.

Pinkerton
Wonderful.

Ufficiale
Posterità.

The Registrar *(to Pinkerton)*
The best of luck.

Pinkerton
Mi proverò.

Pinkerton
I'm much obliged.

Sharpless and the Commissioner and the Registrar depart.

Sharpless
Giudizio!

Sharpless *(returning)*
Be judicious!

Pinkerton
(Ed eccoci in famiglia.)
Sbrighiamoci al più presto e in modo
onesto.

Pinkerton *(to himself)*
(And now I'm with the family.)
Now to get rid of them quickly and in an
honest way.

Pinkerton offers a toast to the guests.

Ip! Ip!   Hip! Hip!

Coro   **Chorus** *(toasting)*
O Kami! o Kami!   O Kami! O Kami!

Pinkerton   **Pinkerton**
Beviamo ai novissimi legami.   Let's drink to new bonds.

Yakusidé, Coro   **Yakusidé, Chorus**
O Kami! o Kami!   O Kami! O Kami!

Pinkerton   **Pinkerton**
beviamo ai novissimi legami.   Let's drink to new bonds.

La Cugina, La Madre   **Cousin, The Mother**
Beviamo, beviamo!   Let's drink! Let's drink!

La Cugina, La Madre, Coro   **A Cousin, The Mother, Chorus**
O Kami! o Kami!   O Kami! O Kami!
Beviamo ai novissimi legami.   Let's drink to new bonds.

The toasts are interrupted by shouting in the distance.

Bonzo   **The Bonze**
Cio-cio-san! Cio-cio-san!   Cio-cio-san! Cio-cio-san!
Abbominazione!   Abomination!

Butterfly, Coro   **Butterfly, Chorus**
Lo zio Bonzo!   It's the uncle Bonze!

Goro   **Goro** *(annoyed)*
Un corno al guastafeste!   A plague on this intruder!
Chi ci leva d'intorno le persone moleste?   Who brought him here to make trouble?

Bonzo   **The Bonze** *(raging)*
Cio-cio-san! Cio-cio-san!   Cio-cio-san! Cio-cio-san!
Cio-cio-san! Cio-cio-san!   Cio-cio-san! Cio-cio-san!
Che hai tu fatto alla Missione?   What were you doing at the Mission?

Parenti ed Amici e la Cugina   **Chorus and the Cousin**
Rispondi, Cio-cio-san!   Answer him, Cio-cio-san!

Pinkerton   **Pinkerton**
Che mi strilla quel matto?   What's that lunatic shrieking?

Bonzo
Rispondi, che hai tu fatto?

The Bonze
Answer him, what were you doing?

Parenti ed Amici
Rispondi, Cio-cio-san!

Friends and relations
Answer him, Cio-cio-san!

Bonzo
Come, hai tu gli occhi asciutti?
Son dunque questi i frutti?
Ci ha rinnegato tutti!

The Bonze
How then have you erred?
These then are the fruits of evil?
She has renounced us all!

Coro
Hou! Cio-cio-san!

Chorus *(scandalized)*
Hou! Cio-cio-san!

Bonzo
Rinnegato vi dico il culto antico.

The Bonze
She has renounced our ancient religion.

Coro
Hou! Cio-cio-san!

Chorus
Hou! Cio-cio-san!

Butterfly hides her face. Her mother comes forward to protect her, but the Bonze pushes her away roughly. He approaches Butterfly in a fury, and shouts into her face.

Bonzo
Kami sarundasico!

The Bonze
Kami sarundasico!

Coro
Hou! Cio-cio-san!

Chorus
Hou! Cio-cio-san!

Bonzo
All'anima tua guasta qual supplizio
sovrasta!

The Bonze
May your wicked soul perish in everlast-
ing torment!

Pinkerton
Ehi, dico: basta, basta!

Pinkerton *(impatiently)*
Be silent now, do you hear me!

Bonzo
Venite tutti. Andiamo!

Ci hai rinnegato e noi.

The Bonze
All come with me. Let's go!
(to Butterfly)
You have renounced us all.

Yakuside e Bonzo, Coro e Cugina
Ti rinneghiamo!

Yakuside, The Bonze, Chorus, Cousin
We renounce you!

Pinkerton
Sbarazzate all'istante. In casa mia
niente baccano e niente bonzeria.

Pinkerton *(ordering all to depart)*
Leave this place immediately. I'll have no
turmoil and disturbance in my house.

Coro
Hou! Cio-cio-san!

Chorus
Hou! Cio-cio-san!

*All rush hastily towards the path which leads down to the town: Butterfly's mother
again tries to approach her, but she is dragged away by the others.*

Renunciation theme:

Bonzo, Yakuside, Coro
Kami sarundasico

The Bonze, Yakuside, Chorus
Kami sarundasico!

Coro
Hou! Cio-cio-san!

Chorus
Hou! Cio-cio-san!

Bonzo, Yakuside, Coro
Ti rinneghiamo!

The Bonze, Yakuside, Chorus
We all renounce you!

*By degrees the voices grow faint in the distance. Butterfly remains motionless and
silent, her face buried in her hands. Pinkerton goes to the top of the path to make sure
that all the troublesome guests have gone.
Butterfly bursts into childish tears, and Pinkerton anxiously tries to console her.*

Pinkerton
Bimba, bimba, non piangere per gracchiar
di ranocchi.

Pinkerton
Dearest, my dearest, don't weep, for they
rant and rave like croaking frogs.

Coro
Hou! Cio-cio-san!

Chorus *(in the distance)*
Hou! Cio-cio-san!

Butterfly
Urlano ancor!

Butterfly *(covering her ears)*
They're still shouting!

Pinkerton
Tutta la tua tribù e i Bonzi tutti del
Giappon non valgono il pianto di quegli
occhi cari e belli.

Pinkerton *(consoling her)*
All your tribes and all the Bonzes in
Japan are not worth a tear from those dear
little beautiful eyes of yours.

Butterfly
Davver?
Non piango più.
E quasi del ripudio non mi duole per le
vostre parole che mi suonan così dolci nel
cor.

Butterfly *(smiling with pleasure)*
Indeed?
I won't cry anymore.
And I'm hardly grieved at their repudia-
tion, because of your sweet comforting
words that sound so sweet in my heart.

Pinkerton
Che fai? La man?

(She stoops to kiss Pinkerton's hand)
Pinkerton *(gently stops her]*
What are you doing? My hand?

Butterfly
M'han detto che laggiù fra la gente
costumata è questo il segno del maggior
rispetto.

Butterfly
They've told me that abroad among the
more cultured people that this is a token
of the highest honor.

Suzuki
E Izaghi ed Izanami
sarundasico, e Kami,
e Izaghi ed Izanami
sarundasico, e Kami.

Suzuki *(murmuring inside the house)*
And Izaghi and Izanami
sarundasico, and Kami
and Izaghi and Izanami
sarundasico, and Kami.

Pinkerton
Chi brontola lassù?

Pinkerton
Who's murmuring in there?

Butterfly
È Suzuki che fa la sua preghiera seral.

Butterfly
It's Suzuki offering her evening prayer.

(evening descends)

Andantino calmo
PINKERTON

Vie - ne - la se - ra,

Pinkerton
Viene la sera.

Pinkerton
Evening is falling.

Butterfly
E l'ombra e la quiete.

Butterfly
With shadows and the tranquility.

Pinkerton
E sei qui sola.

Pinkerton
And you're here alone.

Butterfly
Sola e rinnegata!
Rinnegata, e felice!

Butterfly
Alone and renounced!
Renounced, and happy!

Pinkerton
A voi, chiudete.

Pinkerton *(ordering Suzuki)*
You, come here.

Butterfly
Sì, sì, noi tutti soli.
E fuori il mondo.

Butterfly
Yes, we are all alone.
And away from the world.

Pinkerton
E il Bonzo furibondo.

Pinkerton *(laughing)*
And your furious uncle Bonze!

Butterfly
Suzuki, le mie vesti.

Butterfly
Suzuki, bring my garments.

*Assisted by Suzuki, Butterfly carefully performs her toilet for the night,
and changes her wedding-garment for one of pure white.*

Suzuki
Buona notte.

Suzuki *(bows to Pinkerton)*
Goodnight, Sir.

Butterfly
Quest'obi pomposa di scioglier mi tarda,
si vesta la sposa di puro candor.
Tra motti sommessi sorride e mi guarda.
Celarmi potessi! ne ho tanto rossor!

Butterfly
I long to be rid of this ponderous obi;
a bride must be robed in white garments.
His smiles and looks are caressing.
I can't hide it! I'm blushing!

Pinkerton
Con moti di scojattolo i nodi allenta e
scioglie!
Pensar che quel giocattolo è mia moglie.
Mia moglie!
Ma tal grazia dispiega, ch'io mi struggo
per la febbre d'un subito desìo.

Pinkerton
Her pretty movements are just like a little
squirrel!
And to think that this pretty plaything
is my wife! My wife!
But her charm is so alluring that I struggle
with my feverish, passionate desire.

Butterfly
E ancor l'irata voce mi maledice.
Butterfly rinnegata.
Rinnegata, e felice.

Butterfly
I hear his angry cursing..
Butterfly renounced.
renounced, and happy.

Pinkerton
Bimba dagli occhi pieni di malìa ora sei
tutta mia.
Sei tutta vestita di giglio.
Mi piace la treccia tua bruna fra candidi
veli.

Pinkerton
Little child with eyes full of charm, now
you are mine.
You're fully clad in lily white.
I love your brown hair flowing on your
snowy garment.

Butterfly
Somiglio la Dea della luna, la piccola Dea
della luna che scende la notte dal ponte
del ciel.

Butterfly
I am like the Moon Goddess, the little
Moon-Goddess who comes down by
night from her bridge in the sky.

Pinkerton
E affascina i cuori.

Butterfly
E li prende, e li avvolge in un bianco
mantel.
E via se li reca negli alti reami.

Pinkerton
Ma intanto finor non m'hai detto,
ancor non m'hai detto che m'ami.
Le sa quella Dea le parole
che appagan gli ardenti desir?

Butterfly
Le sa. Forse dirle non vuole per tema
d'averne a morir, per tema d'averne a
morir!

Pinkerton
Stolta paura, l'amor non uccide ma dà
vita, e sorride per gioie celestiali
come ora fa nei tuoi lunghi occhi ovali.

Butterfly
Adesso voi siete per me l'occhio del
firmamento.
E mi piaceste dal primo momento che vi
ho veduto.

Pinkerton
And inflames hearts.

Butterfly
Then she takes them, and she wraps them
in a mantle of white.
And away she bears them, to realms above.

Pinkerton
But you have not told me.
You haven't told me yet that you love me.
Do you think that the Goddess knows the
sweet words I yearn to hear?

Butterfly
She knows, but perhaps will not say them,
for fear that she may die of her love,
for fear she may die of her love!

Pinkerton
Foolish fear, for love does not bring
death, but life and heavenly joy, as now
when it radiates and shines in your eyes.

Butterfly
But now, beloved, you are the eye of the
heavens to me.
And I felt it the very first moment that I
saw you.

Butterfly suddenly panics and covers her ears as if she still hears her relatives
shouting; then she rallies and once more turns confidingly to Pinkerton.

Siete alto, forte.
Ridete con modi si palesi!
E dite cose che mai non intesi.
Or son contenta, or son contenta.

You are so tall, strong.
Your laugh is generous and hearty!
And you say things that are so understand-
ing. I am so happy. I am so happy.

Butterfly
Vogliatemi bene, un bene piccolino,
un bene da bambino quale a me si
conviene, vogliatemi bene.
Noi siamo gente avvezza alle piccole cose
umili e silenziose, ad una tenerezza
sfiorante e pur profonda come il ciel,
come l'onda del mare.

Butterfly
Love me gently, gently like a little one,
like a child, and only let me please you.
Love me gently.
We are simple people accustomed to little
things; humble and quiet like a tender
flower, but as profound as the sky, or the
waves of the oceans.

Pinkerton
Dammi ch'io baci le tue mani cari.
Mia Butterfly!
Come t'han ben nomata tenue farfalla.

Butterfly
Dicon ch'oltre mare se cade in man
dell'uom, ogni farfarla da uno spillo è
trafitta ed in tavola infitta!

Pinkerton
Un po' di vero c'è. E tu lo sai perchè?
Perchè non fugga più. Io t'ho ghermita.
Ti serro palpitante.
Sei mia.

Butterfly
Sì, per la vita.

Pinkerton
Vieni, vieni...
Via dall'anima in pena l'angoscia paurosa.

È notte serena!
Guarda: dorme ogni cosa!

Pinkerton
Give me your darling hands that I may kiss
them. My Butterfly!
How aptly your name was chosen.

Butterfly *(fearfully)*
They say across the seas that if a butterfly
falls into a man's hand, he'll pierce its heart
with a needle, and then leave it to perish!

Pinkerton
There's some truth in that. And do you
know why? That you may not escape.
I have caught you. I hold you as you
flutter. You are mine.

Butterfly
Yes, for life.

Pinkerton
Come, then, come then...
Rid your soul of its fearful anguish.

It is a serene evening!
Look: everything sleeps!

Andante mosso appassionato
BUTTERFLY and PINKERTON

È not - te se - re - na!   Guarda: dorme ogni co - sa!

Butterfly
Ah! Dolce notte!

Pinkerton
Vieni, vieni.

Butterfly
Quante stelle!
Non le vidi mai sì belle!

Butterfly
Ah! Gentle night!

Pinkerton
Come then, come then.

Butterfly
So many stars!
I have never seen it so beautiful!

Pinkerton
È notte serena!
Ah! vieni, vieni.
È notte serena!..
Guarda: dorme ogni cosa!

Butterfly
Dolce notte! Quante stelle!

Pinkerton
Vieni, vieni!

Butterfly
Non le vidi mai sì belle!

Pinkerton
Vieni, vieni!

Butterfly
Trema, brilla ogni favilla.

Pinkerton
Vien, sei mia!

Butterfly
Col baglior d'una pupilla. Oh!
Oh! quanti occhi fisi, attenti
d'ogni parte a riguardar!
pei firmamenti, via pei lidi, via pel mare.

Pinkerton
Via l'angoscia dal tuo cor!
Ti serro palpitante.
Sei mia.
Ah! Vien, vien sei mia
Ah! Vieni, guarda: dorme ogni cosa!
Ti serro palpitante.
Ah, vien!

Butterfly
Ah! quanti occhi fisi, attenti!
quanti sguardi!

Pinkerton
Guarda: dorme ogni cosa:
Ah! Vien! Ah! Vieni, vieni!

Pinkerton
It is a serene evening!
Ah! Come, come!
It is a serene evening!
Look: everything is sleeping!

Butterfly
Gentle night! So many stars!

Pinkerton
Come, come!

Butterfly
I have never seen it so beautiful!

Pinkerton
Come, come!

Butterfly
Every star sparkles and flickers.

Pinkerton
Come, you are mine!

Butterfly
Like a fiery eye flashing. Oh!
Oh! So many eyes in the heavens to
watch us!
They light our path and guard us.

Pinkerton
Cast all fear from your heart!
I feel your heart pulsating.
You are mine.
Ah! Come, come you are mine.
Ah! Come, look at how everything sleeps!
I feel your heart pulsating.
Ah, come!

Butterfly
Oh how gentle the heavens are, how they
are shining!

Pinkerton
Look: everything sleeps.
Ah! Come! Ah! Come, come!.

Ah! Vien. Ah! Vien, sei mia!
Ah! Vien!

Ah! Come! Ah, Come, you are mine!
Ah! Come!

Butterfly
Ride il ciel!
Ah! Dolce notte!
Tutto estatico d'amor
ride il ciel!

Butterfly
Heaven is laughing!
Ah! Gentle night!
Love is ecstatic
and the heavens smile!

Butterfly and Pinkerton enter the house.

ACT II

Inside Butterfly's House

Suzuki
E Izaghi ed Izanami,
Sarundasico e Kami.
Oh! la mia testa!
E tu Ten-Sjoo-daj
fate che Butterfly non pianga più, mai
più, mai più!

Butterfly
Pigri ed obesi son gli Dei Giapponesi!
L'americano Iddio son persuasa
ben più presto risponde a chi l'implori.
Ma temo ch'egli ignori che noi stiam qui di
casa.

Butterfly
Suzuki, è lungi la miseria?

Suzuki
Questo è l'ultimo fondo.

Butterfly
Questo? Oh! Troppe spese!

Suzuki
S'egli non torna e presto, siamo male in
arnese.

Butterfly
Ma torna.

Suzuki
Tornerà!

Butterfly
Perché dispone che il Console provveda
alla pigione, rispondi, su!
Perché con tante cure
la casa rifornì di serrature,
s'ei non volessi ritornar mai più?

Suzuki *(praying)*
And Izaghi and Izanami,
Sarundasico and Kami.
My head is throbbing!
And you, Ten-Sjoo-daj!
Grant me that Butterfly shall weep no
more, no more, no more!

Butterfly
The gods of Japan are fat and lazy.
The American God is more persuasive
and responds immediately to prayers.
But I fear he doesn't know that we are
here in this house.

Butterfly
Suzuki, How soon till we'll be starving?

Suzuki *(shows her a few coins)*
This is all that we have left.

Butterfly
This? Oh, we have been spendthrifts!

Suzuki
Unless he comes, and quickly,
our plight is a bad one.

Butterfly *(decisively)*
But he'll return.

Suzuki *(negatively)*
He'll return?

Butterfly *(reasoning)*
Why did he order the Consul to provide
this house for us? Answer!
Why was he so careful to have the house
provided with safe locks, if he did not
intend to come back?

Suzuki
Non lo so.

Suzuki
I don't know

Butterfly
Non lo sai?
Io te lo dico. Per tener ben fuori le
zanzare, i parenti ed i dolori e dentro, con
gelosa custodia, la sua sposa, la sua sposa
che son io, Butterfly.

Butterfly *(annoyed at her ignorance)*
You don't know?
Then I'll tell you. It was to keep away my
relations, those spiteful scavengers who
might annoy me; and inside it was to give
his wife protection, his wife Butterfly.

Suzuki
Mai non s'è udito di straniero marito
che sia tornato al suo nido.

Suzuki
I never yet heard of a foreign husband
who did return to his nest.

Butterfly
Ah! Taci, o t'uccido.
Quell'ultima mattina:tornerete signor?
gli domandai.
Egli, col cuore grosso, per celarmi la pena
sorridendo rispose:
"O Butterfly piccina mogliettina,
tornerò colle rose alla stagion serena
quando fa la nidiata il pettirosso."
Tornerà.

Butterfly *(furious and seething)*
Ah! Silence, or I'll kill you.
Why, just before he went, I asked him:
you'll come back again to me?
And he answered, with his generous
heart, and concealing his pain:
"Oh Butterfly my tiny little child-wife,
I'll return with the roses, during the warm
sunny season when the robins are nesting."
He'll return.

Suzuki
Speriam.

Suzuki
Let's hope so.

Butterfly
Dillo con me:
Tornerà.

Butterfly *(insisting)*
Say it with me.
He'll return.

Suzuki
Tornerà.

Suzuki *(reluctantly and then in tears)*
He'll return.

Butterfly
Piangi? Perché? Perché?
Ah la fede ti manca!
Senti.

Butterfly
You cry? Why? Why?
Ah you're lacking faith!
Listen to me.

Andante molto calmo
BUTTERFLY

Un   bel di ve - dre-mo   le var - si un fil di fu - mo,

Un bel dì, vedremo levarsi un fil di fumo
sull'estremo confin del mare.
E poi la nave appare.
Poi la nave bianca entra nel porto, romba
il suo saluto.
Vedi? È venuto!

One beautiful day, we will see a thread of
smoke arising on the sea in the far
horizon,
And then a ship appears. Then the trim
white vessel enters the harbor, and
thunders its cannon. You see it? It has come!

Io non gli scendo incontro. Io no.
Mi metto là sul ciglio del colle e aspetto,
e aspetto gran tempo e non mi pesa,
la lunga attesa.

I don't go to meet him. Not I!
I stay there on the hill and I wait, and I
wait for a long time, but it does not weary
me.

E uscito dalla folla cittadina
un uomo, un picciol punto s'avvia per la
collina.
Chi sarà? Chi sarà?
E come sarà giunto che dirà?
che dirà?
Chiamerà Butterfly dalla lontana.
Io senza dar risposta me ne starò nascosta
un po' per celia e un po' per non morire
al primo incontro, ed egli alquanto in
pena chiamerà, chiamerà:
Piccina mogliettina
olezzo di verbena, i nomi che mi dava al
suo venire.

And from out of the crowded city,
a man, a little speck in the distance climbs
the hill.
Can you guess who it is? Who it is?
And when he's reached the summit,
Can you guess what he'll say?
He'll call: "Butterfly" from the distance.
I won't answer and I'll hide myself, a bit
to tease him and a bit so as not to die
from our first meeting. And then a little
pained, he'll call, he'll call:
"Dear baby wife of mine,
dear little orange blossom!" the names he
used to call me when he was here.

Tutto questo avverrà, te lo prometto.
Tienti la tua paura, io con sicura
fede l'aspetto.

This will all happen, I promise you.
Banish your fears, for I await him with
firm faith.

As Butterfly and Suzuki embrace emotionally,
Goro and Sharpless appear in the garden.

Goro
C'è. Entrate.

Goro
She's here. Go in.

Sharpless
Chiedo scusa...Madama Butterfly.

Sharpless
I am seeking...Madam Butterfly.

Butterfly
Madama Pinkerton. Prego.
Oh! Il mio signor Console, signor Console!

Butterfly
Madam Pinkerton, excuse me.
Oh! The Consul, the Consul!

Sharpless
Mi ravvisate?

Butterfly
Ben venuto in casa americana.

Sharpless
Grazie.

Butterfly
Avi, antenati tutti bene?

Sharpless
Ma spero.

Butterfly
Fumate?

Sharpless
Grazie.
Ho qui...

Butterfly
Signore, io vedo il cielo azzurro.

Sharpless
Grazie...
Ho...

Butterfly
Preferite forse le sigarette
Americane?

Sharpless
Ma grazie.
Ho da mostrarvi...

Butterfly
A voi.

Sharpless
Mi scrisse Mister Pinkerton.

Butterfly
Davvero! È in salute?

Sharpless *(surprised)*
You remember me?

Butterfly
Welcome to an American home.

Sharpless
Thank you.

Butterfly
Your honorable ancestors are well?

Sharpless *(smiling)*
I hope so.

Butterfly
You smoke?

Sharpless *(accepts and produces a letter)*
Thank you.
I've here...

Butterfly *(interrupting him)*
Sir. The sky is quite blue.

Sharpless *(refusing a pipe from Suzuki)*
Thank you...
I've here...

Butterfly
Would you perhaps prefer a cigarette?
American?

Sharpless
Well, thank you.
I have to show you...

Butterfly
A light?

Sharpless
I've a letter from Mister Pinkerton.

Butterfly *(with intense eagerness)*
Really! Is he in good health?

Sharpless
Perfetta.

Sharpless
He's quite well.

Butterfly
Io son la donna più lieta del Giappone.
Potrei farvi una domanda?

Butterfly *(joyfully)*
I am the happiest woman in Japan.
Would you answer a question for me?

Sharpless
Certo.

Sharpless
Gladly.

Butterfly
Quando fanno il lor nido in America i
pettirossi?

Butterfly
At what time of the year do the robins
nest in America?

Sharpless
Come dite?

Sharpless *(amazed)*
What did you say?

Butterfly
Sì, prima o dopo di qui?

Butterfly
Yes, sooner or later than here?

Sharpless
Ma, perchè?

Sharpless
Tell me, why?

(Goro, from the garden, eavesdrops on their conversation.)

Butterfly
Mio marito m'ha promesso di ritornar
nella stagion beata che il pettirosso rifà la
nidiata.
Qui l'ha rifatta per ben tre volte, ma può
darsi che di là usi nidiar men spesso.

Butterfly
My husband gave his promise that he would
return in the joyous season when robin
redbreasts rebuild their nests.
Here they have built them three times
already, but I thought that over there it was
less often.

(Goro laughs from outside)

Chi ride?
Oh, c'è il nakodo.

Who's laughing?
Oh, the nakodo.
(whispering to Sharpless)

Un uom cattivo.

A wicked fellow.

Goro
Godo.

Goro *(coming forward and bowing)*
At your pleasure.

Butterfly
Zitto.
Egli osò.
No, prima rispondete alla dimanda mia.

Butterfly
Quiet!*(to Sharpless)*
He's so daring.
No, first answer my question.

Sharpless
Mi rincresce, ma ignoro.
Non ho studiato ornitologia,

Sharpless (*embarassed*)
I apologize for my ignorance.
I never studied ornithology.

Butterfly
orni...

Butterfly
orni...

Sharpless
...tologia.

Sharpless
...tologia

Butterfly
Non lo sapete insomma.

Butterfly
Then you can't tell me either.

Sharpless
No.
Dicevamo...

Sharpless
No.
We were saying...

Butterfly
Ah, sì. Goro,
appena F. B. Pinkerton fu in mare
mi venne ad assediare con ciarle e con
presenti per ridarmi ora questo, or quel
marito.
Or promette tesori per uno scimunito.

Butterfly
Ah, yes, Goro.
As soon as Pinkerton went to sea he came
to me and plagued me with proposals and
gifts, and urged me to consider a marriage
with this one or that one.
Like promises and gifts from an idiot.

Goro
Il ricco Yamadori.
Ella è povera in canna. I suoi parenti
l'han tutti rinnegata.

Goro
The wealthy Yamadori.
She is in a wretched condition. Her
relatives have renounced her.

Butterfly
Eccolo. Attenti.

Butterfly
Here he is. Look.

*Yamadori enters with great pomp, followed by his servants: Goro and Suzuki run up
to him eagerly and kneel before him.
Yamadori greets the Consul, and then bows graciously to Butterfly.*

Butterfly
Yamadori ancor le pene
dell'amor, non v'han deluso?
Vi tagliate ancor le vene se il mio bacio vi
ricuso?

Butterfly
Yamadori, once more has the pain of
unrequited love deluded you?
As you said before, will you end your life
if I refuse your kiss?

Yamadori
Tra le cose più moleste è l'inutil
sospirar.

Yamadori (*to Sharpless*)
Among those troublesome things it is
useless to sigh.

Butterfly
Tante mogli omai toglieste, vi doveste
abituar.

Yamadori
L'ho sposate tutte quante e il divorzio mi
francò.

Butterfly
Obbligata.

Yamadori
A voi però giurerei fede costante.

Sharpless
(Il messaggio, ho gran paura, a trasmetter
non riesco.)

Goro
Ville, servi, oro, ad Omara un palazzo
principesco.

Butterfly
Già legata è la mia fede.

Goro e Yamadori
Maritata ancor si crede.

Butterfly
Non mi credo: sono, sono.

Goro
Ma la legge.

Butterfly
Io non la so.

Goro
Per la moglie, l'abbandono al divorzio
equiparò.

Butterfly
La legge giapponese, non già del mio
paese.

Butterfly
You've had so many wives to become
accustomed to.

Yamadori
I've married all of them and won freedom
through divorce.

Butterfly
Very flattering.

Yamadori
But to you of course I would swear my
faith forever.

Sharpless
(I fear that I will not get far in transmit-
ting this letter.)

Goro
He'll give her houses, servants, money,
and a prince's palace in Omara.

Butterfly
But I am already married.

Goro and Yamadori
She still believes she is married.

Butterfly
You don't believe me, I am, I am.

Goro
But the law.

Butterfly
It's not in force.

Goro
When a wife has been abandoned it is
equivalent to divorce.

Butterfly
The Japanese law does not apply in my
country.

Goro
Quale?

Butterfly
Gli Stati Uniti.

Sharpless
(Oh, l'infelice!)

Butterfly
Si sa che aprir la porta
e la moglie cacciar per la più corta
qui divorziar si dice.
Ma in America questo non si può.
Vero?

Sharpless
Vero. Però..

Butterfly
Là un bravo giudice serio, impettito
dice al marito:
"Lei vuol andarsene?
Sentiam perché?"
"Sono seccato del coniugato!"
E il magistrato:
"Ah, mascalzone, presto in prigione!"

Suzuki, il thè.

Yamadori
Udiste?

Sharpless
Mi rattrista una sì piena cecità.

Goro
Segnalata è già la nave di Pinkerton.

Yamadori
Quand'essa lo riveda...

Sharpless
Egli non vuol mostrarsi. Io venni appunto
per levarla d'inganno.

Goro
Which?

Butterfly
The United States.

Sharpless
(Oh, what a pity!)

Butterfly
One knows that here when a man decides
to turn his wife out at whim, it's automati-
cally a divorce.
But in America that could never happen.
True?

Sharpless
True. Although..

Butterfly
There a good and impartial judge says to
the husband:
"You want to leave?
Why do you feel that way?"
"I am tired of matrimony!"
And the judge replies:
"Ah, scoundrel, immediately to prison!"

Suzuki, the tea.

Yamadori *(whispering to Sharpless)*
Did you hear that?

Sharpless
I'm saddened by so much blindness.

Goro
Pinkerton's ship will soon arrive.

Yamadori
The moment that she sees him....

Sharpless
He doesn't want to see her. I came
expressly to explain her misunderstanding.

Butterfly
Vostra Grazia permette.
Che persone moleste!

Butterfly
Will Your Honor permit me.
What a bothersome person!

Yamadori
Addio. Vi lascio il cuor, pien di
cordoglio: ma spero ancor.

Yamadori
Goodbye. I leave you my heart, full of
sorrow but yet I have hope.

Butterfly
Padrone.

Butterfly
Your privilege.

Yamadori
Ah! se voleste...

Yamadori
Ah! If you were only willing.

Butterfly
Il guaio è che non voglio.

Butterfly
Too bad I'm not willing.

Yamadori bows to Sharpless and departs sighing. Goro eagerly follows Yamadori.
Sharpless becomes grave and serious as he once again invites Butterfly to be seated,
and once more draws the letter from his pocket.

Sharpless
Ora a noi. Sedete qui, legger con me
volete questa lettera?

Sharpless
And now, sit here. Would you like to read
this letter with me?

Butterfly
Date.

Sulla bocca...

sul cuore...

Siete l'uomo migliore del mondo.

Butterfly
Show me.
(kisses the letter)
On my lips...
(placing it on her heart)
on my heart...
(to Sharpless)
You're the best man in the world!

Butterfly returns the letter to Sharpless and settles herself to listen.

Incominciate.

Begin.

Sharpless
"Amico, cercherai quel bel fior di
fanciulla."

Sharpless
"My friend, seek out that beautiful
flower."

Butterfly
Dice proprio così?

Butterfly
Did he really say that?

Sharpless
Sì, così dice, ma se ad ogni momento...

Butterfly
Taccio, taccio, più nulla.

Sharpless
"Da quel tempo felice, tre anni son passati."

Butterfly
Anche lui li ha contati!

Sharpless
"E forse Butterfly non mi rammenta più."

Butterfly
Non lo rammento?
Suzuki, dillo tu.
"Non mi rammenta più!"

Sharpless
(Pazienza!)
"Se mi vuol bene ancor, se m'aspetta."

Butterfly
Oh le dolci parole!
Tu, benedetta!

Sharpless
"A voi mi raccomando perchè vogliate
con circospezione prepararla."

Butterfly
Ritorna.

Sharpless
.....al colpo..."

Butterfly
Quando?
Presto! Presto!

Sharpless
(Benone).
Qui troncarla conviene.
(Quel diavolo d'un Pinkerton!)

Sharpless
Yes, he did, but if at every moment...

Butterfly
I'll be quiet, quiet, no more.

Sharpless
"Since that happy time, three years have passed."

Butterfly
He has counted also!

Sharpless
"And perhaps Butterfly has forgotten me."

Butterfly
I forgot him?
Suzuki, tell him.
"Has forgotten me!"

Sharpless (*to himself*)
(Patience!)
"If she thinks of me, if she is waiting."

Butterfly
Oh what sweet words! (*kisses the letter*)
Blessed letter!

Sharpless
"I recommend that to prepare her you be
circumspect."

Butterfly
He's coming.

Sharpless
....the shock..."

Butterfly
When?
Quickly! Quickly!

Sharpless
(Enough.)
I can spare her no longer.
(That devil Pinkerton!)

Ebbene, che fareste, Madama Butterfly...
s'ei non dovesse ritornar più mai?

Well, what would you do if he should never
return to you?

Butterfly
Due cose potrei far:
tornar, a divertir
la gente col cantar,
oppur, meglio, morire.

Butterfly
I can do two things:
return to entertain the people
with my songs...
or, better, to die.

Sharpless
Di strapparvi assai mi costa dai miraggi
ingannatori.
Accogliete la proposta di quel ricco
Yamadori.

Sharpless
I'm sorry to destroy all of your deceptive
illusions.
But you should accept the wealthy
Yamadori's proposal.

Butterfly
Voi, voi, signor, mi dite questo! Voi?

Butterfly
You, even you tell me that! You?

Sharpless
Santo Dio, come si fa?

Sharpless
Dear God, what can I do?

Butterfly
Qui, Suzuki, presto presto,
che Sua Grazia se ne va.

Butterfly
Suzuki, here, quickly, quickly.
Show His Honor the door.

Sharpless
Mi scacciate?

Sharpless
You dismiss me?

Butterfly
Ve ne prego, già l'insistere non vale.

Butterfly *(changing her mind)*
Please forgive me, but your words
have upset me.

Sharpless
Fui brutale, non lo nego.

Sharpless
I was cruel, I don't deny it.

Butterfly
Oh, mi fate tanto male, tanto male, tanto,
tanto! Niente, niente!

Butterfly
Oh, you have wounded me, wounded me so
deeply! Nothing, nothing!

Ho creduto morir.
Ma passa presto come passan le nuvole
sul mare.

I was sure I was dying.
But it passed quickly as the clouds pass on
the sea.

Ah! M'ha scordata?

Ah! He has forgotten me?

(Butterfly fetches her son)

Butterfly
E questo? E questo? E questo egli potrà
pure scordare?

Sharpless
Egli è suo?

Butterfly
Chi vide mai a bimbo del Giappon occhi
azzurrini?
E il labbro? E i ricciolini d'oro schietto?

Sharpless
È palese.
E Pinkerton lo sa?

Butterfly
No. No.
È nato quand'egli stava
in quel suo gran paese.
Ma voi, gli scriverete che l'aspetta
un figlio senza pari!
e mi saprete dir s'ei non s'affretta
per le terre e pei mari!

Sai cos'ebbe cuore di pensare quel
signore?

Butterfly:
And this baby? This baby? Can he forget
this treasure?

Sharpless
He is his?

Butterfly
Who ever saw a Japanese child with blue
eyes?
And his lips? And his fair golden hair?

Sharpless
It is obvious.
Does Pinkerton know?

Butterfly
No. No.
He was born when my husband was away
in his great country.
But you will write him that he's the father
of a son without equal!
And when he knows he will hasten over
land and sea!
(*to the child*)
Do you know what His Honor has been
thinking in his heart?

Andante molto mosso
BUTTERFLY

Che   tua   ma - dre   do - vrà pren-der -ti in brac - cio,

Che tua madre dovrà
prenderti in braccio ed alla pioggia e al
vento andar per la città a guadagnarti il
pane e il vestimento.

Ed alle impietosite genti, la man tremante
stenderà!
gridando: "Udite, udite la triste mia
canzon.A un infelice madre la carità,
muovetevi a pietà!"

That your mother should take you in her
arms and wander through the city in the
biting wind and blinding rain, begging for
food and clothing.

And extend her hand in supplication to
those impious people!
And shout: "Listen, listen to the sad song
of an unhappy mother and have mercy
and pity her grief."

E Butterfly, orribile destino, danzerà per
te! E come fece già.

And Butterfly's horrible destiny is to
dance for you! As she did before.

La Ghesha canterà!
E la canzon giuliva e lieta in un
singhiozzo finirà!

The Geisha will sing again!
And the happy song will end in a
brokenhearted sigh!

Ah! No! No! Questo mai!
Questo mestier che al disonore porta!
Morta! Morta! Mai più danzar!
Piutosto la mia vita vo' troncar!
Ah! Morta!

But no! No! No! Never!
Not that work of dishonor!
Death! Death! But never dance again!
I'd rather go to my death!
Ah! Death!
(She hugs the child passionately.)

Sharpless
(Quanta pietà!)
Io scendo al piano.
Mi perdonate?

Sharpless *(tearful and emotional)*
(So pitiful!)
I must be going.
You will excuse me?

Butterfly
A te, dagli la mano.

Butterfly *(to the child)*
Now you give him your hand, love.

Sharpless
I bei capelli biondi!

Caro: come ti chiamano?

Sharpless *(takes the child in his arms)*
What beautiful blond hair!
(kisses him)
Darling, what is your name?

Butterfly
Rispondi:
Oggi il mio nome è *Dolore.* Però
dite al babbo, scrivendogli, che il giorno
del suo ritorno,
Gioia, Gioia mi chiamerò.

Butterfly
Answer him!
Today my name now is *Trouble,* but when
my father writes to tell of the day he will
return,
Joy, Joy shall be my name.

Sharpless
Tuo padre lo saprà, te lo prometto.

Sharpless
Your father shall be told, I promise you.

Suzuki
Vespa! Rospo maledetto!

Suzuki *(shouting from outside)*
Scoundrel! Rascal! Wretched coward!

As Sharpless departs, Suzuki drags in Goro.

Butterfly
Che fu?

Butterfly
Who's that?

Suzuki
Ci ronza intorno il vampiro! E ogni giorno
ai quattro venti spargendo va che niuno sa
chi padre al bimbo sia!

Suzuki
He buzzes around here from morning to
evening spreading this scandal that no
one knows who the baby's father is!

Goro
Dicevo, solo, che là in America
quando un figliolo è nato maledetto
trarrà sempre reietto la vita fra le genti!

Goro (protesting and frightened)
I only said that in America when a baby is
born in such shame he will be rejected
and treated as an outcast!

Butterfly
Ah! Tu menti! Menti! Menti!
Ah! menti!

Dillo ancora e t'uccido!

Butterfly (wildly)
Ah! You're lying! Lies! Lies!
Ah! Lies!
[Butterfly threatens to kill him)
Say it again and I'll kill you!

Suzuki
No!

Suzuki (stopping her)
No!

Butterfly
Va via!

Butterfly
Go away!

Butterfly
Vedrai, piccolo amor,
mia pena e mio conforto,
mio piccolo amor.
Ah! Vedrai che il tuo vendicator
ci porterà lontano, lontan, nella sua terra,
lontan ci porterà.

Butterfly (turning to her child)
You see, my adored little love,
my grief, and yet my comfort,
my little love,
Ah! You will see your avenger soon,
and he'll take us far, far off to his land,
far off to his land.

A cannon shot is heard from the harbor.

Suzuki
Il cannone del porto!
Una nave da guerra.

Suzuki
The cannon from the harbor!
A battleship!

Butterfly and Suzuki run to the terrace.

Butterfly
Bianca, bianca, il vessillo americano
delle stelle. Or governa
per ancorare.

Butterfly
White, white... the American stars
and stripes! It's putting into
port to anchor!

Butterfly takes a telescope and directs it to the harbor.

Reggimi la mano ch'io ne discerna
il nome, il nome, il nome. Eccolo:
ABRAMO LINCOLN!

Keep my hand steady so I can read
the name, The name, Where is it? Here it
is: ABRAHAM LINCOLN!

Tutti han mentito! Tutti! Tutti!
sol io lo sapevo sol io che l'amo.

They all were liars! Liars! Liars!
But I knew it always because I love him!

Vedi lo scimunito tuo dubbio?
È giunto! È giunto! È giunto!
Proprio nel punto che ognun diceva;
piangi e dispera.
Trionfa il mio amor!
il mio amor; la mia fè trionfa intera.
Ei torna e m'ama!

Now do you see the folly of doubting?
He's arrived! He's arrived! He's arrived!
Just at the moment you all were saying:
weep and forget him.
My love has triumphed!
My love, my faith has triumphed com-
pletely. He's returned, and he loves me!

Scuoti quella fronda di ciliegio e
m'innonda di fior.
Io vo' tuffar nella pioggia odorosa
l'arsa fronte.

Shake that cherry tree till every snow-
white flower flutters down.
I want him to be showered and smothered
with sweet aromas

Suzuki
Signora, quetatevi, quel pianto.

Suzuki
My lady, be calm, this weeping.

Butterfly
No: rido, rido!
Quanto lo dovremo aspettar?
Che pensi? Un'ora?

Butterfly
No. I am laughing, laughing!
When may we expect him?
What do you think? In an hour?

Suzuki
Di più.

Suzuki
Too soon.

Butterfly
Due ore forse.

Butterfly
Two hours more likely.

Tutto tutto sia pien di fior, come la notte è
di faville.
Va pei fior!

Flowers, flowers must be everywhere, as
many as the stars in the night sky.
Fetch flowers!

Suzuki
Tutti i fior?

Suzuki
Every flower?

Butterfly
Tutti i fior, tutti, tutti.
Pesco, vïola, gelsomin, quanto di cespo,
o d'erba, o d'albero fiorì.

Butterfly
Every flower, all, all.
Peaches, violets, jasmine.
Every bud and blossom from every tree.

Suzuki
Uno squallor d'inverno sarà tutto il
giardin.

Butterfly
Tutta la primavera voglio che olezzi qui.

Suzuki
Uno squallor d'inverno sarà tutto il
giardin.
A voi signora.

Butterfly
Cogline ancora.

Suzuki
Soventi a questa siepe veniste a riguardare
lungi, piangendo nella deserta immensità.

Butterfly
Giunse l'atteso, nulla più chiedo al mare;
diedi pianto alla zolla, essa i suoi fior mi
dà.

Suzuki
Spoglio è l'orto.

Butterfly
Spoglio è l'orto?
Vien, m'aiuta.

Suzuki
Rose al varco della soglia.

Suzuki
The garden will appear desolate like
winter.

Butterfly
I want all of spring's sweetness in here.

Suzuki
The garden will appear desolate like
winter.
Here's more, my lady.

Butterfly
It's not enough yet.

Suzuki
How often you stood here in your vigil of
waiting, weeping to the deserted beyond.

Butterfly
I no longer need to pray, since the kind
sea has brought him. I gave tears to the
earth and it returned flowers to me!

Suzuki
Not a flower left.

Butterfly
Not a flower left?
Come and help me.

Suzuki
Roses shall adorn the threshold.

They scatter flowers everywhere.

Butterfly
Tutta la primavera...

Suzuki
Tutta la primavera...

Butterfly
voglio che olezzi qui....

Suzuki
voglio che olezzi qui....

Butterfly
The breath of spring....

Suzuki
The breath of spring...

Butterfly
I want fragrance here....

Suzuki
I want fragrance here...

Butterfly
Seminiamo intorno april.

Suzuki
Seminiamo intorno april.

Butterfly
Seminiamo april.

Butterfly
Tutta la primavera, voglio che olezzi
qui...

Suzuki
Tutta la primavera, tutta, tutta.
Gigli? Viole?

Butterfly
Intorno, intorno spandi.

Suzuki
Seminiamo intorno april.

Butterfly
Seminiamo intorno april.
Il suo sedil s'inghirlandi,
di convolvi s'inghirlandi;
gigli e viole intorno spandi,
seminiamo intorno april!

Suzuki
Gigli, rose spandi,
tutta la primavera,
spandi gigli, viole,
seminiamo intorno april!

Butterfly
Let us sow April all around.

Suzuki
Let us sow April all around.

Butterfly
Sow April here.

Butterfly
The breath of spring, I want fragrance
here...

Suzuki
The breath of spring, all, all.
Lilies? Violets?

Butterfly
All around, scatter flowers.

Suzuki
Let us sow April all around.

Butterfly
Let us sow April all around.
Garlands on his chair
meshed and entwined.
Let's scatter lilies and violets,
Let's sow April all around!

Suzuki
Scatter lilies and roses,
full of springtime;
Scatter lilies and violets,
Let's sow April all around!

Allegretto moderato
BUTTERFLY and SUZUKI

Ge - tia - mo a ma - ni   pie - ne   mammole e tu - be - ro - se,

Butterfly, Suzuki
Gettiamo a mani piene
mammole e tuberose,
corolle di verbene,
petali d'ogni fior!
Corolle di verbene,
petali d'ogni fior!

Butterfly, Suzuki
We throw handfuls of
violets and white roses,
sprays of sweet verbena,
petals of every flower!
And sprays of sweet verbena,
Petals of every flower!

Butterfly
Or vienmi ad adornar.
No! pria portami il bimbo.

Butterfly
Now come and adorn me.
No, first bring me the baby.

Suzuki fetches the baby and places him next to Butterfly.
Butterfly looks at herself in a hand-mirror and comments sadly.

Non son più quella!
Troppi sospiri la bocca mandò, e l'occhio
riguardò nel lontan troppo fiso.

How much I've changed!
So much sighing has saddened my smile.
And my poor tired eyes have gazed so much!

Dammi sul viso un tocco di carmino.
ed anche a te piccino
perché la veglia non ti faccia vôte
per pallore le gote.

Put a touch of rouge on each cheek
and also on the little one,
because his face is also so pale from all of
the waiting.

Suzuki
Non vi movete che v'ho a ravviare i
capelli.

Suzuki:
Don't move until I've finished setting
your hair.

Butterfly
Che ne diranno ora i parenti!
E lo zio Bonzo?
Già del mio danno tutti contenti!
E Yamadori coi suoi languori!
Beffati, scornati, spennati gli ingrati!

Butterfly: *(laughing at a thought)*
What a surprise for my relations!
And uncle Bonze?
They were all so happy to see my damnation!
And the languorous Yamadori!
His ungrateful airs and scorn!

Suzuki
È fatto.

Suzuki
It is finished.

Butterfly
L'obi che vestii da sposa.
Qua ch'io lo vesta.
Vo' che mi veda indosso il vel del primo
dì.
E un papavero rosso nei capelli.
Così.

Butterfly
My wedding obi.
I want to wear it.
I want him to see me in it like it was on
our wedding day.
And in my hair, we'll put a scarlet poppy.
Like so.

Nello *shosi* farem tre forellini
per riguardar,
e starem zitti come topolini
ad aspettar.

In the *shosi* we'll make three little holes,
that we can look out of.
And we'll be still like little mice and wait
here.

Suzuki closes the shosi screens.
As the night grows darker Butterfly leads the baby to the shosi screen

Butterfly makes three holes in the shosi screen: one at her height, one lower down for
Suzuki, and a third lower still for the child.
She seats the child on a cushion, and indicates that he is to look through the hole.
Suzuki crouches down and also gazes out. Butterfly stands in front of the highest hole
and gazes through it, remaining rigid and motionless as a statue: the baby, who is
between Butterfly and Suzuki, looks out curiously.

The rays of the moonlight illuminate the shosi screen from without. A humming chorus
is heard in the distance from the harbor. The baby falls asleep on a cushion; Suzuki
still in her crouching position, also falls asleep.
Butterfly remains awake, rigid and motionless.

ACT III

Butterfly stands statuesque: the boy sleeps on a cushion with Suzuki next to him.

Marinai
Oh eh! Oh eh!

Sailors *(from the harbor in the distance)*
Oh eh! Oh eh!

(Butterfly rouses herself)

Suzuki
Gia il sole!
Cio-cio-san.

Suzuki
'Tis daylight!
Cio-Cio-San.

Butterfly
Verrà, verrà, col pieno sole.

Butterfly
He'll come, he'll come with daybreak.

Butterfly takes the sleeping child in her arms to bring him to his room.

Suzuki
Salite a riposare, affranta siete
al suo venire vi chiamerò.

Suzuki
Go and rest, you are weary.
I'll call you when he arrives.

Butterfly
Dormi amor mio, dormi sul mio cor.
Tu se con Dio
ed io col mio dolor.
A te i rai degli astri d'or:
Bimbo mio dormi!

Butterfly
Sleep my love, sleep on my heart;
you're safe in God's keeping,
and I with my heavy heart.
Around your head golden stars dart;
sleep, my beloved!

Suzuki
Povera Butterfly!

Suzuki *(sadly, shaking her head)*
Poor Butterfly!

Butterfly
Dormi amor mio, dormi sul mio cor.
Tu sei con Dio
ed io col mio dolor.

Butterfly *(from the room above)*
Sleep my love, sleep on my heart;
you're safe in God's keeping,
and I with my heavy heart.

Suzuki
Povera Butterfly!

Chi sia?

Oh!

Suzuki
Poor Butterfly!
(a light knock at the door)
Who is it?
(Suzuki cries out in great surprise)
Oh!

Sharpless
Stz!

Pinkerton
Zitta!

Suzuki
Zitta!

Pinkerton
Zitta! Zitta!

Pinkerton
Non la destar.

Suzuki
Era stanca sì tanto! Vi stette ad aspettare tutta la notte col bimbo.

Pinkerton
Come sapea?

Suzuki
Non giunge da tre anni una nave nel porto, che da lunge Butterfly non ne scruti il color, la bandiera.

Sharpless
Ve lo dissi?

Suzuki
La chiamo.

Pinkerton
No non ancor.

Suzuki
Lo vedete, ier sera, la stanza volle sparger di fiori.

Sharpless
Ve lo dissi?

Pinkerton
Che pena!

Sharpless (*signals her to be silent*)
Hush!

Pinkerton (*also motions her to be silent*)
Hush!

Suzuki
Hush!

Pinkerton
Hush! Hush!

Pinkerton
Don't disturb her!

Suzuki
She was so very tired! She stood awaiting you all night with the baby.

Pinkerton
How did she know?

Suzuki
For three years, no ship has entered the harbor that Butterfly has not scrutinized for its flags and colors.

Sharpless (*to Pinkerton*)
Didn't I tell you?

Suzuki
I'll call her.

Pinkerton
No, not yet.

Suzuki
Look around you, the room is full with flowers.

Sharpless (*touched*)
Didn't I tell you?

Pinkerton
What torment!

Suzuki
Chi c'è là fuori nel giardino?
Una donna!

Pinkerton
Zitta!

Suzuki
Chi è? Chi è?

Sharpless
Meglio dirle ogni cosa.

Suzuki
Chi è? Chi è?

Pinkerton
È venuta con me.

Suzuki
Chi è? Chi è?

Sharpless
È sua moglie!

Suzuki
Anime sante degli avi!
Alla piccina s'è spento il sol, s'è spento il
sol!

Sharpless
Scegliemmo quest'ora mattutina per
ritrovarti sola, Suzuki, e alla gran prova
un aiuto, un sostegno cercar con te.

Suzuki
Che giova? Che giova?

Sharpless
Lo so che alle sue pene non ci sono
conforti!
Ma del bimbo conviene assicurar le sorti!

Suzuki
Who's that outside in the garden?
A lady!

Pinkerton
Hush!

Suzuki (*becoming more agitated*)
Who's that? Who's that?

Sharpless (*to Pinkerton*)
It's better to tell her everything.

Suzuki
Who's that? Who's that?

Pinkerton (*embarrassed*)
She came with me.

Suzuki
Who's that? Who's that?

Sharpless
She's his wife!

Suzuki (*stupefied*)
Hallowed souls of our fathers!
The sun has set for the fragile Butterfly,
the sun has set!

Sharpless
Suzuki, we decided to come here early in
the morning so we would find you alone,
and that you might help and guide us.

Suzuki (*in despair*)
How can I help? How can I help?

Sharpless
I know that for such misfortune there's no
consolation!
But the child's future welfare must be
secured from a horrible destiny!

Pinkerton
Oh! L'amara fragranza di questi fior,
velenosa al cor mi va.

Sharpless
La pietosa che entrar non osa materna
cura del bimbo avrà.

Suzuki
Oh me trista!
E volete ch'io chieda ad una madre?

Pinkerton
Immutata è la stanza dei nostri amor.

Sharpless
Suvvia, parla, suvvia, parla con quella pia
e conducila qui, s'anche la veda Butterfly,
non importa.
Anzi, meglio se accorta del vero si
facesse alla sua vista.
Suvvia, parla con quella pia,
suvvia, conducila qui,
conducila qui.

Pinkerton
Ma un gel di morte vi sta.

Il mio ritratto.
Tre anni son passati,
tre anni son passati,
tre anni son passati e noverati
n'ha i giorni e l'ore, i giorni e l'ore!

Suzuki
E volete ch'io chieda ad una madre?
Oh! Me trista! Oh! Me trista!
Anime sante degli avi!
Alla piccina s'è spento il sol!
Oh! Me trista!
Anime sante degli avi!
Alla piccina s'è spento il sol!

Pinkerton
Oh! The bitter fragrance of these flowers
is like poison in my heart.

Sharpless
This gentle lady who dare not enter,
will give the child a mother's care.

Suzuki
Oh what sadness!
And you want me to tell a mother?.

Pinkerton
This room of our past love is unchanged.

Sharpless
Don't delay, talk to her, don't delay,
Talk to that gentle lady, and bring her here.
Even if Butterfly should see her, no matter.
Then with her own eyes she will learn the
cruel truth that we can't bear to tell her.
Go then, speak with that gentle lady,
go quickly and bring her here,
bring her here.

Pinkerton
But a deathly chill haunts the air.
(sees his picture)
My portrait.
Three years have passed,
three years have passed,
three years have passed and she counted
every hour of every day!

Suzuki
And you want me to tell a mother?
Oh! Woe is me! Oh! My sorrow!
Hallowed souls of my fathers!
Now the sun has set for the fragile woman!
Oh! It grieves me!
Hallowed saints of my fathers!
For the little woman, the sun has set!

Sharpless ushers Suzuki into the garden to join Kate Pinkerton.

Sharpless
Vien, Suzuki, vien!

Pinkerton
Non posso rimaner.

Suzuki
Oh! Me trista!

Pinkerton
Sharpless, v'aspetto per via.

Sharpless
Non ve l'avevo detto?

Pinkerton
Datele voi qualche soccorso.
Mi struggo dal rimorso,
mi struggo dal rimorso.

Sharpless
Vel dissi? Vi ricorda?
quando la man vi diede: "badate!
Ella ci crede" e fui profeta allor!
Sorda ai consigli, sorda ai dubbî,
vilipesa nell'ostinata attesa raccolse il cor.

Pinkerton
Sì, tutto in un istante
io vedo il fallo mio e sento
che di questo tormento
tregua mai non avrò,
mai non avrò! no!

Sharpless
Andate: il triste vero da sola apprenderà.

Sharpless
Go, Suzuki, go!

Pinkerton (*overcome by emotion*)
I cannot remain.

Suzuki (*leaving*)
Oh! It grieves me!

Pinkerton
Sharpless, I'll wait for you outside.

Sharpless
Isn't it as I told you?

Pinkerton (*gives Sharpless money*)
Give her some support.
I struggle with my anguish,
I struggle with my anguish.

Sharpless
I warned you, you remember?
When she gave you her hand: Be careful!
She believed you and was sincere! She
blindly trusted you and gave you her heart;
and you were deaf to advice.

Pinkerton
Yes, in one sudden moment,
I see my heartless faults and sense
that from this torment,
I will always be haunted,
always be haunted!

Sharpless
Go: she should hear the sad truth alone.

Allegro moderato
PINKERTON

Ad - di - o fiorito a - sil,   di le - ti - zia e d'a - mor.

Pinkerton
Addio fiorito asil
di letizia e d'amor.
Sempre il mite suo sembiante
con strazio atroce vedrò.

Pinkerton
Farewell, sanctuary of flowers
and home of love.
I will be haunted forever
by my atrocious guilt.

Sharpless
Ma or quel cor sincero presago è già..

Sharpless
Dark omens are already forecast.

Pinkerton
Addio fiorito asil.

Pinkerton
Farewell, sanctuary of flowers.

Sharpless
Vel dissi, vi ricorda?
E fui profeta allor.

Sharpless
I warned you... you remember?
It was my prophesy.

Pinkerton
Non reggo al tuo squallor,
Ah! Non reggo al tuo squallor!
Fuggo, fuggo, son vil!
Addio, non reggo al tuo squallor.

Pinkerton
I cannot bear my guilt.
Ah! I cannot bear to stay in this squalor!
I must flee, I must flee, I am vile!
Farewell, I cannot bear my guilt.

Sharpless
Andate, il triste vero apprenderà.

Sharpless
Yes go, and let her learn the sad truth.

Pinkerton
Ah! Non reggo, son vil!

Pinkerton
Ah! I cannot bear it, I am vile!

As Pinkerton exits quickly, Kate and Suzuki enter from the garden.

Kate
Glielo dirai?

Kate *(compassionately to Suzuki)*
Then will you tell her?

Suzuki
Prometto.

Suzuki
I promise.

Kate
E le darai consiglio d'affidarmi?

Kate
And will you advise her to trust me?

Suzuki
Prometto.

Suzuki
I promise.

Kate
Lo terrò come un figlio.

Kate
I'll care for him as if he was my own son.

Suzuki
Vi credo. Ma bisogna ch'io le sia sola
accanto.
Nella grande ora, sola! Piangerà tanto
tanto! Piangerà tanto!

Suzuki
I believe you. But I must be quite alone at
her side.
In this cruel hour, alone! She'll weep so
sadly! She'll weep so sadly!

Butterfly
Suzuki!

Butterfly *(calling from the room above)*
Suzuki!

Suzuki!
Dove sei?
Suzuki!

Suzuki!
Where are you?
Suzuki!

Suzuki
Son qui, pregavo e rimettevo a posto.

Suzuki
I'm here... I was praying, and going back
to watch.

Suzuki tries to prevent Butterfly from descending the stairs.

No...
no... no... no... no... non scendete...
no... no... no.

No...
no... no... no... no... Do not come down...
no... no... no.

Butterfly
È qui... è qui... dove è nascosto?
È qui... è qui.

Butterfly *(excitedly)*
He's here... he's here... where is he
hidden? He's here... he's here.

Ecco il Console.

(noticing Sharpless)
Here's the Consul.
(searching for Pinkerton)

E dove? Dove?
Non c'è!

and... where is he?... where is he?
Not here!

Chi siete?
Perchè veniste?
Niuno parla!

(sees Kate and looks at her fixedly)
Who are you?
Why have you come here?
No one answers!
(to Suzuki)

Perché piangete?

Why are you weeping?
(Butterfly becomes frightened)

No, non ditemi nulla... nulla... forse
potrei cader morta sull'attimo.

No, no, tell me nothing... nothing...for I
might die the moment I hear it.
(affectionately to Suzuki)

Tu Suzuki che sei tanto buona, non
piangere! E mi vuoi tanto bene un sì, un
no, di' piano. Vive?

You, Suzuki, are always so good, don't
weep! Since you love me so dearly,
say "yes," or "no," quite softly. He lives?

Suzuki
Sì.

Butterfly
Ma non viene più. Te l'han detto!

Vespa! Voglio che tu risponda.

Suzuki
Mai più.

Butterfly
Ma è giunto ieri?

Suzuki
Sì.

Butterfly
Ah! Quella donna mi fa tanta paura! Tanta paura!

Sharpless
E la causa innocente d'ogni vostra sciagura. Perdonatele.

Butterfly
Ah! È sua moglie.
Tutto è morto per me!
tutto è finito! Ah!

Sharpless
Coraggio!

Butterfly
voglion prendermi tutto!
Il figlio mio!

Sharpless
Fatelo pel suo bene il sacrifizio.

Butterfly
Ah! Triste madre! Triste madre!
Abbandonar mio figlio!
E sia! A lui devo obbedir!

Suzuki
Yes.

Butterfly *(transfixed)*
But he is not coming. They have told you!
(angered at Suzuki's silence)
Viper! I want you to reply!

Suzuki
No more.

Butterfly
But he arrived yesterday?

Suzuki
Yes.

(understanding, she looks at Kate warily)
Butterfly
That lady that terrifies me! She terrifies me!

Sharpless
She is the innocent cause of your trouble. Forgive her.

Butterfly
Ah! She is his wife.
All is over for me!
All is finished! Ah!

Sharpless
Courage!

Butterfly
You'll take everything from me!
My child!

Sharpless
They will give him the most loving care.

Butterfly *(despairingly)*
Ah! Sad mother! Sad mother!
To abandon my son!
So be it! For him I must obey!

Kate
Potete perdonarmi, Butterfly?

Butterfly
Sotto il gran ponte del cielo non v'è donna di voi più felice.

Siatelo sempre, non v'attristate per me.

Kate
Povera piccina!

Sharpless
È un immensa pietà!

Kate
E il figlio lo darà?

Butterfly
A lui lo potrò dare se lo verrà a cercare.

Fra mezz'ora salite la collina.

Kate
Are you able to forgive me, Butterfly?

Butterfly *(solemnly)*
Beneath the arches of heaven there is no woman happier than you are.

Remain that way forever, and never feel sorry for me.

Kate
Poor little woman!

Sharpless
It's an immense pity!

Kate
And you'll give him his son?

Butterfly
I will give him his son if he will come to take him.
In a half hour, he can climb this hill.

Suzuki escorts Kate and Sharpless out.
Butterfly almost collapses, and Suzuki hastens to support her.

Suzuki
Come una mosca prigioniera l'ali batte il piccolo cuor!

Butterfly
Troppa luce è di fuor, e troppa primavera. Chiudi.

Il bimbo ove sia?

Suzuki
Giuoca. Lo chiamo?

Butterfly
Lascialo giuocar, lascialo giuocar.
Va a fargli compagnia.

Suzuki
Resto con voi.

Suzuki
This trembling heart beats like an imprisoned, frightened bird!

Butterfly
The room is too bright, and too full of springtime. Make it darker!

Where is the baby?

Suzuki
Playing. Shall I call him?

Butterfly *(anguished)*
Let him play. let him play.
Go keep him company.

Suzuki *(tearfully)*
I'll stay with you.

Butterfly
Va, va. Te lo comando.

Butterfly *(with resolution)*
Go, go. I command you!

Butterfly lights the lamp on the shrine of the Buddha. She removes a white veil and a dagger. She piously kisses the blade and reads its inscription.

"Con onor muore chi non può serbar vita con onore."

"To die with honor for one who cannot serve life with honor."

The door opens, and Suzuki's arm is seen pushing the child towards his mother. The boy runs to Butterfly with outstretched hands. Butterfly lets the dagger fall, and passionately hugs and kisses him.

Butterfly
Tu? Tu? Tu? Tu tu? Tu? Tu?
piccolo Iddio! Amore, amore mio,
fior di giglio e di rosa.
Non saperlo mai per te,
per toui puri occhi,
muor Butterfly..
perchè tu possa andar di lè dal mare
sensa chi ti rimorda ai dì maturi il
materno abbandono.

Butterfly
You? You? You? You? You? You? You?
Little god! My adored one, my love,
fairest lily and rose.
You must never know,
in your pure eyes,
that Butterfly died and abandoned you so
you could go to another land beyond the
sea, and never know when you grow older
of her devotion.

O a me,   sce - so   dal tro - no   del l'al-tro Pa - ra - di - so,

O a me. sceso dal trono del l'alto
Paradiso,
guarda ben fiso, fiso di tua madre la
faccia!
Che t'n resti una traccia,
guarda ben!
Amore, addio, addio! Piccolo amor!
Va Gioca, gioca.

My son, sent to me from Paradise,
look well at your mother's features,
that it's memory may remain,
Look well!
Beloved, goodbye, goodbye, dearest love!
Go, play, play!

Butterfly gives the child an American flag and a doll. Then she bandages his eyes.
With her eyes still fixed upon the boy, she goes behind the screen.
The dagger is heard falling to the ground. Butterfly emerges from behind the screen,
groping for the child while she smiles feebly. She drags the child toward her, having
just enough strength to embrace him. Then she falls to the ground.

Pinkerton arrives and is heard calling.

Butterfly! Butterfly! Butterfly!

Pinkerton and Sharpless rush into the room. Butterfly points to the child and dies.
Pinkerton falls to his knees while Sharpless tenderly embraces the child.

MADAMA BUTTERFLY

Discography

1939   Dal Monte (Butterfly); Gigli (Pinkerton);
         Basiola (Sharpless); Palombini (Suzuki);
         Rome Opera Chorus and Orchestra;
         Fabritis (Conductor)

1940   (Live Metropolitan Opera performance)
         Albanese (Butterfly); Melton (Pinkerton); Brownlee (Sharpless);
         Metropolitan Opera Chorus and Orchestra;
         Cimara (Conductor)

1949   Steber (Butterfly); Tuckers (Pinkerton);
         Valdengo (Sharpless); Madeira (Suzuki);
         Metropolitan Opera Chorus and Orchestra;
         Rudolf (Conductor)

1951   Illitsch (Butterfly); Delorco (Pinkerton);
         Gligor (Sharpless); Rössi-Majdan (Suzuki);
         Austrian State Opera;
         Loibner (Conductor)

1951   Tebaldi (Butterfly); Campora (Pinkerton);
         Inghilleri (Sharpless); Rankin (Suzuki);
         Academy of Santa Cecilia Chorus and Orchestra;
         Erede (Conductor)

1953   Frati (Butterfly); Taddei (Pinkerton);
         Giorgetti (Sharpless); Bertolini (Suzuki);
         Florence Festival Chorus and Orchestra;
         Ghiglia (Conductor)

1954   Petrella (Butterfly); Tagliavini (Pinkerton);
         Taddei (Sharpless); Masini (Suzuki);
         Turin Radio Chorus and Orchestra;
         Questa (Conductor)

1954   De los Angeles (Butterfly); di Stefano (Pinkerton);
         Gobbi (Sharpless); Canali (Suzuki);
         Rome Opera Chorus and Orchestra;
         Gavazzeni (Conductor)

1955   Callas (Butterfly); Gedda (Pinkerton);
         Boriello (Sharpless); Danieli (Suzuki);
         La Scala Chorus and Orchestra;
         Von Karajan (Conductor)

1956   (in French)
        Angelici (Butterfly); Lance (Pinkerton);
        Giovanetti (Sharpless); Collard (Suzuki);
        Opéra-Comique Chorus and Orchestra;
        Wolff (Conductor)

1958   Moffo (Butterfly); Valletti (Pinkerton);
        Cesari (Sharpless); Elias (Suzuki);
        Rome Opera Chorus and Orchestra;
        Leinsdorf (Conductor)

1959   Tebaldi (Butterfly); Bergonzi (Pinkerton);
        Sordello (Sharpless); Cossotto (Suzuki);
        Academy of Santa Cecilia Chorus and Orchestra;
        Serafin (Conductor)

1960   (in German)
        Schlemm (Butterfly); Kónya (Pinkerton);
        Borg (Sharpless); Plümacher (Suzuki);
        Württemberg State Opera Chorus and Orchestra;
        Leitner (Conductor)

1960   De los Angeles (Butterfly); Björling (Pinkerton);
        Sereni (Sharpless); Pirazzini (Suzuki);
        Rome Opera Chorus and Orchestra;
        Santini (Conductor)

1962   Price (Butterfly); Tuckers (Pinkerton);
        Maero (Sharpless); Elias (Suzuki);
        Rome Opera Chorus and Orchestra;
        Leinsdorf (Conductor)

1966   Gordoni (Butterfly); Molese (Pinkerton);
        Meucci (Sharpless); Sacei (Suzuki);
        Vienna State Opera Chorus and Orchestra;
        Santi (Conductor)

1966   Scotto (Butterfly); Bergonzi (Pinkerton);
        Panerai (Sharpless); Stasio (Suzuki);
        Rome Opera Chorus and Orchestra;
        Barbirolli (Conductor)

1969   Kabaivanska (Butterfly); Taddei (Pinkerton);
        Maffeo (Sharpless); Marcossi (Suzuki);
        Naples Academy Chorus/Naples Philharmonic Orchestra;
        Rapalo (Conductor)

1971   Chiara (Butterfly); King (Pinkerton);
        Prey (Sharpless); Schmidt (Suzuki);
        Munich Bavarian Radio Chorus and Orchestra;
        Patané (Conductor)

1974   Freni (Butterfly); Pavarotti (Pinkerton);
        Kerns (Sharpless); Ludwig (Suzuki);
        Vianna State Opera Chorus/Vienna Philharmonic Orchestra;
        Von Karajan (Conductor)

1976   Caballé (Butterfly); Martí (Pinkerton);
        Bordoni (Sharpless); Mazzieri (Suzuki);
        Barcelona Liceo Theatre Chorus/Barcelona Symphony Orchestra;
        Gatto (Conductor)

1978   Scotto (Butterfly); Domingo (Pinkerton);
        Wixell (Sharpless); Knight (Suzuki);
        Ambrosian Opera Chorus/Philharmonia Orchestra;
        Maazel (Conductor)

1980   Kineses (Butterfly); Dvorsky (Pinkerton);
        Miller (Sharpless); Takács (Suzuki);
        Hungarian State Opera Chamber Chorus/Hungarian State Opera Orchestra;
        Patané (Conductor)

198(?) Kabaivanska (Butterfly); Antinori (Pinkerton);
        Portella (Sharpless); Milcheva-Nonova (Suzuki);
        Bulgarian National Choir/Sofia Philharmonic Orchestra;
        Bellini (Conductor)

1988   Freni (Butterfly); Carreras (Pinkerton);
        Pons (Sharpless); Berganza (Suzuki);
        Ambrosian Opera Chorus/Philharmonic Orchestra;
        Sinopoli (Conductor)

MADAMA BUTTERFLY

Videography

Virgin VHS
>Hayashi (Butterfly); Dvorsky (Pinkerton);
>Zancanaro (Sharpless); Kim (Suzuki);
>La Scala Chorus and Orchestra;
>Maazel (Conductor)
>Asari (Director)
>Bailey (Video Director)

Castle VHS
>Kabaivanska (Butterfly); Antinori (Pinkerton);
>Saccomani (Sharpless); Jankovic (Suzuki);
>Verona Arena Chorus and Orchestral
>Arena (Conductor);
>Chazaletes (Director)
>Large (Video Director)

Decca VHS
>Freni (Butterfly); Domingo (Pinkerton);
>Kerns (Sharpless); Ludwig (Suzuki);
>Vienna State Opera Choir/Vienna Philharmonic Orchestra;
>Von Karajan (Conductor)
>A film by Jean-Pierre Ponnelle

Erato Films
>Presented by Martin Scorcese
>Huang (Butterfly); Troxell (Pinkerton);
>Choeur de Radio France/Orchestra de Paris;
>Conlon (Conductor)
>A Film by Frederic Mitterand

DICTIONARY OF OPERA AND MUSICAL TERMS

Accelerando - Play the music faster, but gradually.

Adagio - At slow or gliding tempo, not as slow as Largo, but not as fast as Andante.

Agitato - Restless or agitated.

Allegro - At a brisk or lively tempo, faster than Andante but not as fast as Presto.

Andante - A moderately slow, easy-going tempo.

Appoggiatura - An extra or embellishing note preceding a main melodic note or tone. Usually written as a note of smaller size, it shares the time value of the main note.

Arabesque - Flourishes or fancy patterns usually applying to vocal virtuosity.

Aria - A solo song usually structured in a formal pattern. Arias generally convey reflective and introspective thoughts rather than descriptive action.

Arietta - A shortened form of aria.

Arioso - A musical passage or composition having a mixture of free recitative and metrical song.

Arpeggio - Producing the tones of a chord in succession but not simultaneously.

Atonal - Music that is not anchored in traditional musical tonality; it uses the chromatic scale impartially, does not use the diatonic scale and has no keynote or tonal center.

Ballad Opera - 18th century English opera consisting of spoken dialogue and music derived from popular ballad and folksong sources. The most famous is *The Beggar's Opera* which was a satire of the Italian opera seria.

Bar - A vertical line across the stave that divides the music into units.

Baritone - A male singing voice ranging between the bass and tenor.

Baroque - A style of artistic expression prevalent in the 17th century that is marked generally by the use of complex forms, bold ornamentation, and florid decoration. The Baroque period extends from approximately 1600 to 1750 and includes the works of the original creators of modern opera, the Camerata, as well as the later works by Bach and Handel.

Bass - The lowest male voices, usually divided into categories such as:

> **Basso buffo -** A bass voice that specializes in comic roles like Dr. Bartolo in Rossini's *The Barber of Seville*.

> **Basso cantante** - A bass voice that demonstrates melodic singing quality rather than comic or tragic: King Philip in Verdi's *Don Carlos*.

> **Basso profundo -** the deepest, most profound, or most dramatic of bass voices: Sarastro in Mozart's *The Magic Flute*.

Bel canto - Literally "beautiful singing." It originated in Italian opera of the 17th and 18th centuries and stressed beautiful tones produced with ease, clarity, purity, evenness, together with an agile vocal technique and virtuosity. Bel canto flourished in the first half of the 19th century in the works of Rossini, Bellini, and Donizetti.

Cabaletta - Typically a lively bravura extension of an aria or duet that creates a climax. The term is derived from the Italian word "cavallo," or horse: it metaphorically describes a horse galloping to the finish line.

Cadenza - A flourish or brilliant part of an aria commonly inserted just before a finale.

Camerata - A gathering of Florentine writers and musicians between 1590 and 1600 who attempted to recreate what they believed was the ancient Greek theatrical synthesis of drama, music, and stage spectacle; their experimentation led to the creation of the early structural forms of modern opera.

Cantabile - An expression indication urging the singer to sing sweetly.

Cantata - A choral piece generally containing Scriptural narrative texts: Bach Cantatas.

Cantilena - A lyrical melodic line meant to be played or sung "cantabile," or with sweetness and expression.

Canzone - A short, lyrical operatic song usually containing no narrative association with the drama but rather simply reflecting the character's state of mind: Cherubino's "Voi che sapete" in Mozart's *The Marriage of Figaro*. Shorter versions are called canzonettas.

Castrato - A young male singer who was surgically castrated to retain his treble voice.

Cavatina - A short aria popular in the 18th century without the da capo repeat section.

Classical Period - The period between the Baroque and Romantic periods. The Classical period is generally considered to have begun with the birth of Mozart (1756) and ended with Beethoven's death (1830). Stylistically, the music of the period stressed clarity, precision, and rigid structural forms.

Coda - A trailer or tailpiece added on by the composer after the music's natural conclusion.

Coloratura - Literally colored: it refers to a soprano singing in the bel canto tradition with great agility, virtuosity, embellishments and ornamentation: Joan Sutherland singing in Donizetti's *Lucia di Lammermoor.*

Commedia dell'arte - A popular form of dramatic presentation originating in Renaissance Italy in which highly stylized characters were involved in comic plots involving mistaken identities and misunderstandings. The standard characters were Harlequin and Colombine: The "play within a play" in Leoncavallo's *I Pagliacci.*

Comprimario - A singer portraying secondary character roles such as confidantes, servants, and messengers.

Continuo - A bass part (as for a keyboard or stringed instrument) that was used especially in baroque ensemble music; it consists of a succession of bass notes with figures that indicate the required chords. Also called *figured bass, thoroughbass.*

Contralto - The lowest female voice derived from "contra" against, and "alto" voice, a voice between the tenor and mezzo-soprano.

Countertenor, or male alto vocal range - A high male voice generally singing within the female high soprano ranges.

Counterpoint - The combination of one or more independent melodies added into a single harmonic texture in which each retains its linear character: polyphony. The most sophisticated form of counterpoint is the fugue form in which up to 6 to 8 voices are combined, each providing a variation on the basic theme but each retaining its relation to the whole.

Crescendo - A gradual increase in the volume of a musical passage.

Da capo - Literally "from the top": repeat. Early 17th century da capo arias were in the form of A B A, the last A section repeating the first A section.

Deus ex machina - Literally "god out of a machine." A dramatic technique in which a person or thing appears or is introduced suddenly and unexpectedly; it provides a contrived solution to an apparently insoluble dramatic difficulty.

Diatonic - Relating to a major or minor musical scale that comprises intervals of five whole steps and two half steps.

Diminuendo - Gradually getting softer, the opposite of crescendo.

Dissonance - A mingling of discordant sounds that do not harmonize within the diatonic scale.

Diva - Literally a "goddess"; generally refers to a female opera star who either possesses, or pretends to possess, great rank.

Dominant - The fifth tone of the diatonic scale: in the key of C, the dominant is G.

Dramma giocoso - Literally meaning amusing, or lighthearted. Like tragicomedy it represents an opera whose story combines both serious and comic elements: Mozart's *Don Giovanni.*

Falsetto - Literally a lighter or "false" voice; an artificially produced high singing voice that extends above the range of the full voice.

Fioritura - Literally "flower"; a flowering ornamentation or embellishment of the vocal line within an aria.

Forte, Fortissimo - Forte (*f*) means loud: mezzo forte (*mf*) is fairly loud; fortissimo (*ff*) even louder, and additional *fff*'s indicate greater degrees of loudness.

Glissando - A rapid sliding up or down the scale.

Grand Opera - An opera in which there is no spoken dialogue and the entire text is set to music, frequently treating serious and dramatic subjects. Grand Opera flourished in France in the 19th century (Meyerbeer) and most notably by Verdi (Aida): the genre is epic in scale and combines spectacle, large choruses, scenery, and huge orchestras.

Heldentenor - A tenor with a powerful dramatic voice who possesses brilliant top notes and vocal stamina. Heldentenors are well suited to heroic (Wagnerian) roles: Lauritz Melchoir in Wagner's *Tristan und Isolde.*

Imbroglio - Literally "Intrigue"; an operatic scene with chaos and confusion and appropriate diverse melodies and rhythms.

Largo or larghetto - Largo indicates a very slow tempo; Larghetto is slightly faster than Largo.

Legato - Literally "tied"; therefore, successive tones that are connected smoothly. Opposing Legato would be Marcato (strongly accented and punctuated) and Staccato (short and aggressive).

Leitmotif - A short musical passage attached to a person, thing, feeling, or idea that provides associations when it recurs or is recalled.

Libretto - Literally "little book"; the text of an opera. On Broadway, the text of songs is called "lyrics" but the spoken text in the play is called the "book."

Lied - A German song; the plural is "lieder." Originally German art songs of the 19th century.

Light opera, or operetta - Operas that contain comic elements but light romantic plots: Johann Strauss's *Die Fledermaus.*

Maestro - From the Italian "master": a term of respect to conductors, composers, directors, and great musicians.

Melodrama - Words spoken over music. Melodrama appears in Beethoven's *Fidelio* but flourished during the late 19th century in the operas of Massenet (*Manon*). Melodrama should not be confused with melodrama when it describes a work that is characterized by extravagant theatricality and by the predominance of plot and physical action over characterization.

Mezza voce - Literally "medium voice," or singing with medium or half volume; it is generally intended as a vocal means to intensify emotion.

Mezzo-soprano - A woman's voice with a range between that of the soprano and contralto.

Molto - Very. Molto agitato means very agitated.

Obbligato - An elaborate accompaniment to a solo or principal melody that is usually played by a single instrument.

Octave - A musical interval embracing eight diatonic degrees: therefore, from C to C is an octave.

Opera - Literally "a work"; a dramatic or comic play combining music.

Opera buffa - Italian comic opera that flourished during the bel canto era. Buffo characters were usually basses singing patter songs: Dr. Bartolo in Rossini's *The Barber of Seville,* and Dr. Dulcamara in Donizetti's *The Elixir of Love.*

Opéra comique - A French opera characterized by spoken dialogue interspersed between the arias and ensemble numbers, as opposed to Grand Opera in which there is no spoken dialogue.

Operetta, or light opera - Operas that contain comic elements but tend to be more romantic: Strauss's *Die Fledermaus,* Offenbach's *La Périchole*, and Lehar's *The Merry Widow.* In operettas, there is usually much spoken dialogue, dancing, practical jokes, and mistaken identities.

Oratorio - A lengthy choral work, usually of a religious or philosophical nature and consisting chiefly of recitatives, arias, and choruses but in deference to its content, performed without action or scenery: Handel's *Messiah.*

Ornamentation - Extra embellishing notes—appoggiaturas, trills, roulades, or cadenzas—that enhance a melodic line.

Overture - The orchestral introduction to a musical dramatic work that frequently incorporates musical themes within the work.

Parlando - Literally "speaking"; the imitation of speech while singing, or singing that is almost speaking over the music. It is usually short and with minimal orchestral accompaniment.

Patter - Words rapidly and quickly delivered. Figaro's Largo in Rossini's *The Barber of Seville* is a patter song.

Pentatonic - A five-note scale, like the black notes within an octave on the piano.

Piano - Soft volume.

Pitch - The property of a musical tone that is determined by the frequency of the waves producing it.

Pizzicato - A passage played by plucking the strings instead of stroking the string with the bow.

Polyphony - Literally "many voices." A style of musical composition in which two or more independent melodies are juxtaposed in harmony; counterpoint.

Polytonal - The use of several tonal schemes simultaneously.

Portamento - A continuous gliding movement from one tone to another.

Prelude - An orchestral introduction to an act or the whole opera. An Overture can appear only at the beginning of an opera.

Presto, Prestissimo - Very fast and vigorous.

Prima Donna - The female star of an opera cast. Although the term was initially used to differentiate between the dramatic and vocal importance of a singer, today it generally describes the personality of a singer rather than her importance in the particular opera.

Prologue - A piece sung before the curtain goes up on the opera proper: Tonio's Prologue in Leoncavallo's *I Pagliacci*.

Quaver - An eighth note.

Range - The divisions of the voice: soprano, mezzo-soprano, contralto, tenor, baritone, and bass.

Recitative - A formal device that that advances the plot. It is usually a rhythmically free vocal style that imitates the natural inflections of speech; it represents the dialogue and narrative in operas and oratorios. Secco recitative is accompanied by harpsichord and sometimes with cello or continuo instruments and *accompagnato* indicates that the recitative is accompanied by the orchestra.

Ritornello - A short recurrent instrumental passage between elements of a vocal composition.

Romanza - A solo song that is usually sentimental; it is usually shorter and less complex than an aria and rarely deals with terror, rage, and anger.

Romantic Period - The period generally beginning with the raiding of the Bastille (1789) and the last revolutions and uprisings in Europe (1848). Romanticists generally found inspiration in nature and man. Beethoven's *Fidelio* (1805) is considered the first Romantic opera, followed by the works of Verdi and Wagner.

Roulade - A florid vocal embellishment sung to one syllable.

Rubato - Literally "robbed"; it is a fluctuation of tempo within a musical phrase, often against a rhythmically steady accompaniment.

Secco - The accompaniment for recitative played by the harpsichord and sometimes continuo instruments.

Semitone - A half-step, the smallest distance between two notes. In the key of C, the notes are E and F, and B and C.

Serial music - Music based on a series of tones in a chosen pattern without regard for traditional tonality.

Sforzando - Sudden loudness and force; it must stick out from the texture and provide a shock.

Singspiel - Early German musical drama employing spoken dialogue between songs: Mozart's *The Magic Flute*.

Soprano - The highest range of the female voice ranging from lyric (light and graceful quality) to dramatic (fuller and heavier in tone).

Sotto voce - Literally "below the voice"; sung softly between a whisper and a quiet conversational tone.

Soubrette - A soprano who sings supporting roles in comic opera: Adele in Strauss's *Die Fledermaus*, or Despina in Mozart's *Così fan tutte*.

Spinto - From the Italian "spingere" (to push); a soprano having lyric vocal qualities who "pushes" the voice to achieve heavier dramatic qualities.

Sprechstimme - Literally "speak voice." The singer half sings a note and half speaks; the declamation sounds like speaking but the duration of pitch makes it seem almost like singing.

Staccato - Short, clipped, rapid articulation; the opposite of the caressing effects of legato.

Stretto - A concluding passage performed in a quicker tempo to create a musical climax.

Strophe - Music repeated for each verse of an aria.

Syncopation - Shifting the beat forward or back from its usual place in the bar; it is a temporary displacement of the regular metrical accent in music caused typically by stressing the weak beat.

Supernumerary - A "super"; a performer with a non-singing role: "Spear-carrier."

Tempo - Time, or speed. The ranges are Largo for very slow to Presto for very fast.

Tenor - Highest natural male voice.

Tessitura - The general range of a melody or voice part; but specifically, the part of the register in which most of the tones of a melody or voice part lie.

Tonality - The organization of all the tones and harmonies of a piece of music in relation to a tonic (the first tone of its scale).

Tone Poem - An orchestral piece with a program; a script.

Tonic - The keynote of the key in which a piece is written. C is the tonic of C major.

Trill - Two adjacent notes rapidly and repeatedly alternated.

Tutti - All together.

Twelve tone - The 12 chromatic tones of the octave placed in a chosen fixed order and constituting with some permitted permutations and derivations the melodic and harmonic material of a serial musical piece. Each note of the chromatic scale is used as part of the melody before any other note gets repeated.

Verismo - Literally "truth"; the artistic use of contemporary everyday material in preference to the heroic or legendary in opera. A movement from the late 19th century: *Carmen*.

Vibrato - A "vibration"; a slightly tremulous effect imparted to vocal or instrumental tone for added warmth and expressiveness by slight and rapid variations in pitch.